TWAYNE'S WORLD AUTHORS SERIES
A Survey of the World's Literature

FRANCE

Maxwell A. Smith, Guerry Professor of French, Emeritus
The University of Chattanooga
Former Visiting Professor in Modern Languages
The Florida State University

EDITOR

Maurice Barrès

TWAS 454

Maurice Barrès

MAURICE BARRÈS

By ANTHONY A. GREAVES

University of Calgary

TWAYNE PUBLISHERS
A DIVISION OF G. K. HALL & CO., BOSTON

Library of Congress Cataloging in Publication Data

Greaves, Anthony A
    Maurice Barrès.

    (Twayne's world authors series : TWAS 454)
    Bibliography: p. 165
    Includes index.
    1.   Barrès, Maurice, 1862–1923—Criticism and
Interpretation.
PQ2603.A52Z73   843'.9'12   77–23074
ISBN 0–8057–6291–4

Contents

About the Author

Anthony Greaves was educated in England, and in 1965 obtained a Ph.D. from the University of Nottingham, for a thesis on the life and works of Paul Bonnetain. Since 1963, he has taught French and Spanish in the Department of Romance Studies at the University of Calgary. His publications center mainly on nineteenth century literature, and include studies on Huysmans, Maupassant and Zola.

Preface

Towards the end of his life, Barrès was the acknowledged spokesman of French nationalism. Few of his contemporaries cared to realize that he was much more. Nationalism was just one aspect of a multifaceted personality which seemed to grow richer with the passing years. After his death, the publication of his *Cahiers* softened the sharp edges of his thought. He is now appreciated for his inquiry into the sources of creative energy, and for the haunting poetry of his style.

Barrès himself attempted to present his evolution as a logical growth, from development of one's ego, to development of one's country, to development of humanity in general. He does not explain what impulses lay behind this evolution, but the reasons are there to be uncovered. This study is intended to illuminate the different features of Barrès' writings, and show the connections between them. After an outline of Barrès' life, each chapter will take up an important aspect of his work. The development of these aspects is roughly chronological, although there is inevitably some overlap.

My thanks are due to Maxwell Smith, who aroused my interest in Barrès, and to my colleagues and students, past and present, who through discussion have enabled me to clarify my ideas. Needless to say, the responsibility for errors is mine alone.

ANTHONY A. GREAVES

University of Calgary

Chronology

1862 19th August: birth at Charmes-sur-Moselle.
1873 Entry into the college of La Malgrange.
1877 Entry into the lycée at Nancy.
1880 Has Burdeau as philosophy teacher in the lycée.
1883 First visit to Italy.
1884– Editor of *Les Taches d'encre*.
1885
1888 *Sous l'oeil des barbares*.
1889 *Huit jours chez M. Renan. Un Homme libre*. Elected to Parliament in Nancy on a Boulangist program.
1891 *Le Jardin de Bérénice. Trois stations de psychothérapie*.
1892 *Toute licence sauf contre l'amour*. First visit to Spain. Panama scandal.
1893 *L'Ennemi des lois*. Loses his parliamentary seat in Nancy. Boulangism collapses. Marries Mlle Paule Couche.
1894 *Du Sang, de la Volupté et de la Mort. Une Journée parlementaire*.
1897 *Les Déracinés*.
1898 Loses his contest for a parliamentary seat in Nancy. Death of his father. Second trial of Dreyfus at Rennes.
1899 Visits German-occupied Alsace. Meets Dr. Pierre Bucher.
1900 *L'Appel au Soldat*. 19th April – 25th May: visit to Greece.
1901 Death of his mother. Resigns from the *Ligue de la Patrie Française*.
1902 *Leurs Figures. Scènes et doctrines du nationalisme*. Visits Venice and Toledo.
1903 *Amori et dolori sacrum. Les Amitiés françaises*. Meets Anna de Noailles.
1904 *De Hegel aux cantines du Nord*.
1905 *Au Service de l'Allemagne*.
1906 *Le Voyage de Sparte*. Elected to the *Académie Française*, filling Hérédia's seat. Elected to Parliament by the Parisian constituency of Neuilly-Boulogne, which he represents until his death.

1907 7th December: departure on a four week trip to Egypt.
1909 *Colette Baudoche. Gréco ou le Secret de Tolède.* Death of his nephew, Charles Demange.
1913 *La Colline inspirée.*
1914 *La Grande Pitié des Eglises de France.* Journey through the Middle East. First World War begins.
1917 *Les Diverses Familles spirituelles de la France.*
1920 First volume of *Chronique de la Grande Guerre.* November: gives five lectures at the University of Strasbourg on *Le Génie du Rhin.*
1922 *Un jardin sur l'Oronte.*
1923 *Une enquête aux pays du Levant.* 4th December: dies of a heart attack.
1924 *Faut-il autoriser les Congrégations?*
1925 *Pour la haute intelligence française.*
1926 *Le Mystère en pleine lumière.*
1927 *Les Maîtres.*
1929 First volume of *Mes Cahiers.* After a break due to the war, the last volume (vol. 14) appears in 1948.
1930 *Les Grands Problèmes du Rhin.*
1948 *N'importe où hors du monde.*

CHAPTER 1

The Man

THROUGHOUT its turbulent history, Lorraine has been both a meeting place and a battleground. Barrès possesses in full measure the patriotism and combative spirit formed by the ensuing clash of cultures. Three of his grandparents had long associations with the region. His paternal grandfather, originally from Auvergne, roamed Europe with Napoleon's armies, then retired in 1830 to Charmes-sur-Moselle, the home-town of his wife, whom he had met and married in 1827 while garrisoned at Nancy. In 1859 his son, a respected engineer, married another local girl, Claire-Anne Luxer. The local birth register shows that their son, Auguste-Maurice, was born on 19th August 1862, at one o'clock in the afternoon.

I *Youth and Literary Apprenticeship*

In 1867, Barrès fell victim to a serious attack of typhoid fever. It was starting from this period that his mother began to read to him from the novels of Walter Scott, whose account of Richard the Lion Heart in Palestine set up reverberations that echo to the end of Barrès' life and underscore his attraction to things oriental. The images of Moslem women that filled his young imagination were recreated in the harems of his last novel, *Un jardin sur l'Oronte*.

In 1870, an even more vivid scene impressed itself upon him. After the Prussian invasion, the gaiety and bravery of the French soldiers as they advanced to do battle would remain firmly imprinted in his mind as an ideal which only the French army might attain. The brutality of the German invaders, reinforced by their clockwork precision and blind obedience, would symbolize a degree of barbarity to which only Germans could allow themselves to sink.

11

The object of the attention of a large group of well-meaning relatives, Barrès experienced a happy childhood, until his parents decided to send him to a boarding school with the unprepossessing name of La Malgrange. Nothing had prepared him for the sudden shock he was to experience. He had, on the contrary, looked forward to the event with eager anticipation. When he arrived at the school, everything was as the prospectus had led him to believe. He turned to speak to his parents. They had taken advantage of a moment of inattention to slip away. He was suddenly overwhelmed with a feeling of solitude, which a sense of being different from the other pupils helped to perpetuate. His unhappiness was gradually dulled, but never went away entirely, not even after he left for the more open atmosphere of the lycée in Nancy. A study of the records of the schools Barrès attended suggests that he was a somewhat less than average student. The future master of French prose received a prize for Latin, but never for French.[1] Barrès tended to find comfort in the religious services, which perhaps explains his attraction in later life for the pomp and ceremony of Catholicism and the feeling of peace he thought it could bring.[2]

Barrès suffered from the lack of interest he perceived in his teachers, and even in his parents. They seemed to want him to fit some pre-cast mold of what they thought an adolescent should be, without taking into account his own particular personality and desires.[3] Only one teacher understood him sufficiently well to advise his parents that the young man should be allowed to attempt a career as a writer. Among his unimaginative schoolmates, he discovered Stanilas de Guaïta. Barrès has recounted how de Guaïta, his elder by one year, introduced him to Gautïer, Baudelaire, Flaubert, Heine and Taine.[4] Their works, with which he felt a true kinship, were much more provoking than the monotonous, uninspired teaching of his professors. His companion introduced him into a small circle of equally ardent young men, whose main occupation after class hours seems to have been reading poetry and arguing interminably amid clouds of cigarette smoke and piles of empty coffee cups. Barrès claimed that these discussions with the first companions he had met who shared his view of life, marked him deeply,[5] although to the reader the atmosphere appears vaguely nauseating.

One other individual in the lycée marked Barrès for good. This was Burdeau, professor of philosophy, later minister of the

Marine, and president of the Chamber of Deputies. What he taught was not particularly new, but his powerful personality commanded attention and respect. Although he later reacted violently against everything that Burdeau stood for, Barrès' admiration for the man whose influence never really left him is clearly distinguishable.[6]

We are fortunate in possessing some of the correspondence which passed between Barrès and two of his closest friends, Stanislas de Guaïta and Léon Sorg.[7] The latter took a strong interest in Barrès' welfare and often wrote him letters of encouragement when Barrès was feeling depressed. It took some time for Barrès to achieve an equilibrium between his desire to emulate those masters he admired who had already attained distinction, and the conviction that a young writer ought to break new ground. He turned to one writer after another, not solely to assimilate their knowledge, but in search of new impressions, new methods of investigation, new ways of presenting material.[8] Barrès alternated between optimism and pessimism. His moments of depression, which were usually accompanied by rather severe bouts of illness, would give way to a better balanced realization of his chances for success. After some struggle with his parents, Barrès was at last able to settle permanently in Paris in January 1883, and throw himself into the literary fray.

At this early date, Barrès realized that Naturalism was close to its apogee, and quite apart from the personal distaste he felt for the crudity of many young would-be Naturalists' works, was not inclined to hitch his fortunes to a literary school on the point of decline.[9] According to Jules Renard,[10] Barrès was also attracted to the work of Huysmans who at that time was the outstanding representative of Decadentism and the "fin de siècle." This influence could not touch Barrès for long. He was perceptive enough to realize that, like Naturalism, Decadentism was played out, and that the creator of a new attitude would reap fame and glory. He set out to become a modern interpreter of the French spirit, to show the people what their true genius was. To this end, he studied philosophers and historians, and added Spencer, Renan and Jules Soury[11] to his reading list. He gradually gained more confidence in his powers, and learned to accept — as Sorg had already warned him — that success would come slowly. After a year in Paris, he was able to claim with some satisfaction that although he had not yet reached his goal — a guaranteed position that would pay him a living wage and leave him enough leisure to write — he was well on the way to achieving it.[12] Now that he was not subject to the frustrations of thwarted ambitions, his health stabilized, giving him greater time for composition.

In July 1884, Barrès confided to Léon Sorg his most important undertaking to date, the creation of his own monthly review of which he himself would be editor. He had worked out the costs for each monthly number at about 200 francs, and expected to be able to start with about 300 subscribers paying one franc per copy. Beneath his enthusiasm, however, one can discern his appreciation of the venture as a rather risky excursion into a market already glutted with struggling reviews. His main reason for the undertaking appears unvarnished in his admission to Sorg that regardless of the fate of the review, it would set him apart from his rivals. He expected to make his mark in a year. By the beginning of October, he was certain of little more than one hundred subscribers, although still hopeful of reaching more through a publicity agent. At this rate, the *Taches d'encre was* incompatible with his expensive style of living, and after the fourth issue he allowed it to fold up. His purpose had been achieved, and other reviews were asking him for more articles than he had time to write. He was also cautious about pushing his belligerence too far. To draw attention to himself, he had to play the part of the iconoclastic young man, but to become known just as a scandal-monger would have jeopardized his future. He drew back from the brink, and set about establishing a more solid claim to fame. By the Fall of 1887, Barrès had attained all his objectives. His financial situation was secure, his name was familiar, and his first book was ready for publication. Barrès no longer had doubts over what style to adopt, and simply allowed his thoughts to express themselves naturally. He realized that the originality he sought was already present within himself. From this moment, Barrès would unashamedly put his own thoughts and feelings into his work under only the thinnest of disguises. He himself would become the subject of his books.

II *Political Reform and Literary Innovation*

An apparently insignificant incident in 1885 had a profound bearing on his future career. He had agreed to act as second for Félicien Champsaur in a duel with Robert Caze, a rather quarrelsome journalist, more skilful with a pen than with a sword, who met his death a few months later in yet another duel. Caze had taken legal action against Champsaur, and as second, Barrès was obliged to present himself in court too. Their lawyer was Laguerre, through whom Barrès gained an introduction into the corridors of Boulangism. His first article in support of Boulanger appeared on 14th September 1887 in *Le Voltaire*. Although still a somewhat uncertain movement, Boulangism was a force to be reckoned with. It attracted ambitious men seeking to use Boulanger's popularity to further their own designs. Their argument was that the so-called supporters of the Republic were merely corrupt self-seekers, who took advantage of the parliamentary system to further their own gain. The remedy lay in change, in a dissolution of Parliament and in the installation by popular acclaim of an honest man who would wield the power and authority necessary to clean up the system. In 1889 Barrès, standing as a Boulangist candidate at Nancy, was carried into Parliament on the wave of popular sympathy built up by the Boulanger legend. He was not content, however, to rely wholly upon the prestige of his leader. With his co-workers, he canvassed support, organized meetings, and founded a newspaper, the *Courrier de l'est*. It was purely a political undertaking designed to further his candidacy. Assuming full editorial responsibility, Barrès demonstrated his ever present flair for publicity and developed a style composed of invective and insinuation that often came close to defamation.

The energy Barrès deployed in running his campaign contrasts strangely with the timidity of solutions he proposed to remedy social injustice. His social program could be reduced to four essential points: the establishment of a pension plan for workers, tax reform, protection of French workers from foreign competition, and legal recognition of the rights of unions.[13] Concerning constitutional reform, Barrès echoed Naquet's demands.[14] In constructing a fairly vague, bland program, Barrès followed the lead of the major exponents of Boulangism, who were drawn from so many different factions that they were united only by opposition to the current regime and by Boulanger's own charismatic personality. In later years, whether founding the *Ligue de la Patrie française* or defending French churches, Barrès would refrain from elaborating a coherent program in the interest of attracting as wide a cross section of support as possible. It is not certain whether Barrès' success in 1889 was due solely to his efforts to unite the two large factions of workers and petty bourgeoisie against the small but powerful faction of big business. His failure in 1898, to win in the Nancy constituency on a similar platform, suggests that though his efforts to socialize Boulangism may have been helpful, it was in the end the appeal of Boulanger himself that carried the day.

In this flurry of political activity, Barrès was busy putting the final touches to *Un homme libre,* the second in the *Culte du Moi* trilogy. This novel assured his position as leader of the young generation, attracted by Barrès' cult of energy linked with the freedom to experiment and experience new sensations. Leaving behind the jaded skepticism of his elders, Barrès maintained that it was possible to arouse in oneself enthusiasm for whatever cause one had decided to promote. There were many who considered his interest in politics simply as the dabbling of a dilettante trying to keep himself amused. Events soon proved this criticism to be quite unfounded. When Boulanger refused to press home his advantage and seize power, it led to the collapse of the heterogeneous elements of the party that had formed around him. Rather than waste his time in sterile recrimination, Barrès took the lead in throwing in his lot with the Socialists. He consistently voted in favor of any proposal designed to improve the lot of the working classes, and took a personal hand in drawing up two amendments, one aimed at preventing children from working the night shift, the other to increase the amount of money available for scholarships.

As it turned out, the Boulanger crisis was but the forerunner of a long series of crises the young Republic had to weather. Scarcely a year after Boulanger committed suicide, the Panama scandal broke. In the interval, Barrès had been indulging some of his desires for new, exciting places. Already in 1887, he had been to Italy. He would never forget the impression Venice made upon him. In later years, he would claim that Venice's most important effect was to make him realize the value of his own Lorraine, but nothing of this reaction is present in his first writings on the theme of Italy. He was impressed by the painting, by the culture, but above all by a certain voluptuous languor, a hint of decadent refinement that covered centuries of breeding. Ironically enough, the vigor of a nationalistic Italy, recently united, escaped his attention. What he saw was a cultural heritage which mixed piety, suffering and passion. In 1892, Barrès undertook his first visit to Spain, where he encountered a slightly different type of exoticism in the form of raw passion which battered him into submission, rather than seducing him. The land seemed to be one of violent contrasts, days of heat and blinding light followed by nights of cold and darkness, the piety of the nobles and the cruelty of the Inquisition, the barren harshness of Castile and the softer appeal of Arabic Granada.

III *Outside Parliament*

In 1893, Barrès' role in Parliament came to an end. Sensing that his chances of re-election in Nancy were slim, he presented himself to the constituents of Neuilly-Boulogne, but lost to his opponent. The year brought other compensations, however, for Barrès married Mlle Paule Couche. Freed from Parliamentary commitments, he threw himself with renewed vigor into literature and political organization. One of his works, *Une journée parlementaire,* was inspired by the Panama Scandal. The play presents a corrupt Minister, tangled up in the web of his own deceit, who is eventually hounded to suicide by a vindictive newspaper editor determined to use his indiscretions to avenge a personal affront. Perhaps hoping to play a role akin to that of his fictional editor, Barrès founded *La Cocarde,* a newspaper whose editorial board, somewhat like Boulangism, was distinguished by the union of exponents of apparently irreconcilable doctrines. Anarchists, Socialists, Jews, Protestants, Legitimists — all were united for a time by Barrès.[15]

The paper folded after six months, but while it lasted, it attempted to create a youth movement, particularly among students, in favor of Socialism. In an effort to create as broad an appeal as possible, Barrès proclaimed himself a patriot, a socialist and an anti-Semite,[16] as well as a federalist. The main value of the paper for Barrès lay in the efforts he was obliged to make to crystallize his thoughts for presentation in the articles he composed. He was gradually led to discover himself and clarify tendencies he had previously not suspected. Undoubtedly, one of the strongest influences on him was that of Hegel, and his theory of thesis, antithesis and synthesis. Barrès had already used the method in *Un homme libre* in an attempt to integrate Romanticism and Rationalism to form an instrument for self-development. In *La Cocarde,* he interpreted Hegelianism to mean a process of constant change and development towards an unknown goal.

In 1896, prior to the birth of his son, Philippe, Barrès installed himself and his wife at Neuilly, on the outskirts of Paris. Henri Massis has recalled the somewhat austere atmosphere of this house on the Boulevard Maillot,[17] which was to remain Barrès' home for the rest of his life. He ran for election in the Neuilly riding, but was defeated, despite support from the Socialist block and Jaurès, later to become a political opponent with whom Barrès evolved a curious love-hate relationship. Over the subsequent ten years, Barrès would fail again to gain election to Parliament, but each defeat would merely strengthen his commitment to work for political change from outside the Chamber through a long-term education of the French public into a realization of the necessity of the alterations he proposed.

As he had been well aware when he founded the *Taches d'encre,* articles have an immediate impact, but their effect is quickly forgotten as they are overlaid by other pressing preoccupations. Barrès would never be content with a somewhat facile notoriety. He sought instead the more lasting fame and influence that came through the publication of books. He now began work on the trilogy known under the general title of *Le Roman de l'énergie nationale.* The first of these, *Les Déracinés,* was published in 1897, and immediately caused heated debate. Everyone had something to say concerning the relative merits of "rootedness" and "uprootedness." Drawing a botanical example, André Gide quoted a nursery brochure extolling the exceptional health and vigor of transplanted trees. Others made fun of an exponent of regionalism who had chosen to live in Paris. Barrès rightly shrugged off this rather facile criticism. It does not matter where one lives. Rootedness means an awareness of one's cultural heritage, and it was precisely this that by now was most strong in Barrès. Pressed by Léon Blum, who had been delegated by the Dreyfusards to win him to their cause, Barrès replied that when in doubt, he would rely on his instinct and his nationalist sentiment. Running on a program of nationalism, Socialism and protectionism, he was passed over by the Nancy electorate in favor of a more anti-Semitic opponent. Now, throwing his energies into the fight against Dreyfus' defenders, he gradually dropped Socialism from his program, and concentrated instead on a nationalism summed up in the traditional institutions which continued to flourish. It is claimed that after 1918, he recognized Dreyfus' innocence and regretted having taken such a prominent role in the matter.[18] In his defense, it may be said that for both his attackers and his defenders, Dreyfus was an excuse to pursue the struggle of republicans against reactionaries. In all his writings, Barrès was motivated by what he thought best for his country. In January 1889, Barrès was instrumental in the creation of the *Ligue de la Patrie Française.* Although pressed to assume the presidency, he preferred to cede the place to Jules Lemaître. His reasons for doing so betray an attitude, already apparent in *Un homme libre,* which would influence his actions for the rest of his life. He was wary of any situation which would confine him in an overly narrow system. His nationalism, for example, rested on a broad cultural base, and never degenerated into an attempt to impose restrictions on the traditions of the past. New elements were welcomed, but were transformed to harmonize with a tradition which itself was in a constant process of development. Unlike many of his contemporaries, Barrès did not divide the nation into two sections, one good and the other bad. He recognized that there were good intentions in the majority of people, and he hoped to bring them all together in a party of conciliation. By the same token, he was wary of official administrative positions, recognizing that they could constrict his field of action. He always preferred, whenever possible, to play the role of independent critic, affirming his solidarity with his party's broad principles, but remaining free to criticize the way they were put into effect, if he thought it warranted. Consequently, his relations with Charles Maurras always remained cordial, even though the latter split away from the League to form his own *Action Française,* which confined nationalism to a narrow monarchism that Barrès could not accept.

Although there was a great deal in politics to keep Barrès busy, it occupied only a portion of his life. From 1898 onwards, there were many other preoccupations to beset him. He suffered a great loss at the end of June, when his father died. His past opposition to his son becoming a writer was long forgiven and forgotten. With his last words, he told his son how content he was that he had succeeded so well. Only three years later, on 30th July 1901, his mother died. Barrès' grief was deeply felt. Unlike the Romantics, who imagined every change in their emotions reflected in nature, Barrès was all too aware of the total indifference of the world of things. His whole interior world had changed, yet on the exterior, it remained the same. His sense of loss could not be fully comforted by the thought that she continued to exist in him. For a moment, he

thought of withdrawing completely from politics, the better to
devote himself to her memory.[19] Wiser counsels prevailed, however, as he realized that he could best serve her by being himself and
working for the causes which satisfied his own inner compulsions.
In the spring of 1900, he spent five weeks traveling through
Greece. His reactions were mixed. He found it difficult to assess in
just what way the land and culture had affected him, so that it was
not until 1906 that he actually published his impressions, under the
title *Le Voyage de Sparte.*

In the meantime, in 1903, he had met Anna de Noailles. His first
impression of her had not been at all favorable, and there is more
than a hint of condescension in the way he speaks of this Branco-
van woman who presumed to defend Dreyfus.[20] Very soon, however, it was the foreign qualities, the exoticism of Anna de Noailles
that attracted him. She appeared to be the synthesis of all those
fatal charms he had given to his exotic heroines, Princess Marina of
L'Ennemi des lois, or Astiné Arévian of *Les Déracinés.* His early
memories of Walter Scott and his admiration for the noble ladies
who accompanied Richard the Lion Heart lent an irresistible aura
of romance and yearning to her figure. Whenever she is mentioned
in the *Cahiers,* there is praise for her sensitivity, her genius, her
depth of feeling. Barrès began composing short stories whose
flavor was vaguely oriental, Muslim or Arabic. One of these, *La
Musulmane courageuse,* although not published in Barrès' lifetime,
was used in the composition of *Un jardin sur l'Oronte,* written
many years after Barrès' definitive separation from Mme de
Noailles.

In the summer of 1903, he spent a month with her in Savoy.
There are some suspicions that perhaps Barrès considered a divorce
from his wife at this time[21] but there is little to back up such an
assertion beyond his obvious infatuation for Anna de Noailles, and
his lavish praise of her personality and work. Barrès had never
taken women particularly seriously. His comments in his youthful
letters to Léon Sorg betray this tendency to regard his mistresses as
little more than playthings. He gradually came to see in Mme de
Noailles more undesirable characteristics. She tended to be self-
centered and could be viciously spiteful when her whims were
crossed. Their meetings became less frequent, and they agreed
upon an amicable parting. Unwittingly, Mme de Noailles had given
Barrès a great deal. She not only reawakened his enthusiasm for

exoticism, but she made him keenly aware of the element of the mysterious in life. Disappointed with politics, repeatedly rejected by the electorate, Barrès had undergone a period of depression, out of which Mme de Noailles lifted him. She taught him a new "song of confidence in life"[22] and aroused his interest in the sources of creative spiritual energy, a quest that he was to pursue in France and abroad for the rest of his life.

Barrès was beginning to take a very close interest in the fate of the annexed provinces. In August 1902, he was in Niederbronn, in Alsace, spending sufficient time to gather the preliminary material for use in the novel which was eventually entitled *Au Service de l'Allemagne,* and published in 1905. He had been fortunate enough to meet Dr. Pierre Bucher, a patriot who had stayed behind, in the belief that it was his duty to maintain a French presence in the conquered territory. From Bucher, Barrés, obtained a great deal of information concerning the pressures, legal and otherwise, that the Germans brought to bear in their efforts to absorb the French population. He learned also of the secret struggles of the French minority to preserve their language and culture, and undertook actively to support their efforts. This was not a particularly popular course of action to take. Contrary to what Barrès wished to proclaim, the masses between 1875 and 1914 were mostly against war, and felt no particular enthusiasm for the recuperation of Alsace and Lorraine. This attitude was particularly prevalent in Southern France, leading Barrès to call the Southerners traitors, whose aim was to divide the nation.[23]

As a direct result of his campaign against the South, Barrès' antipathy for Jaurès increased, while his regionalism and federalism were stifled. It also became obvious to him that he would cut a more authoritative figure inside Parliament, and that his polemic would have a greater impact if he appeared as something more than a disgruntled ex-deputy sniping against his former colleagues. Consequently, he stood for a by-election at the end of 1902, and again in April 1903. Despite a fairly powerful following, Barrès failed to be elected each time.

IV   *Spokesman of the Right*

The year 1906 at last recompensed Barrès for the efforts he and his friends had deployed. In January, he was elected to the Académie Française, succeeding to the chair of Hérédia. In May, he was at last elected to Parliament by the first district of Paris. The solidly conservative shopkeepers and petty bourgeois of this district were doubtless flattered to be represented by an "Immortal," for through succeeding re-elections, he was to keep this seat until his death. Opinions on Barrès' influence vary considerably. Contemporary newspaper accounts of his political campaigns claim that he was unable to project an impressive image.[24] Once in Parliament, however, his effectiveness was more marked,[25] despite a rather harsh, almost croaky voice quite lacking in oratorical flight.[26] When they were published, his speeches appeared much more impressive, being designed to be read, rather than spoken. His political influence can be seen as indirect — reaching down through Charles de Gaulle to the present day,[27] — or as direct, on Poincaré and Millerand.[28] Barrès himself was delighted to be back. "I might not think much of the system," he said, "but I enjoy belonging to the club."[29] Recalling Taine's remark to Bourget, that "that young Barrès will never amount to anything much, because he is attracted by two quite irreconcilable tendencies, a taste for meditation and a desire for action,"[30] Barrès claimed that politics had given meaning to his life, by enabling him to effect the impossible reconciliation.[31]

One of his first acts in the Chamber was to intervene in favor of General Mercier, now the target of the triumphant Dreyfus supporters. Barrès did not waste time attempting to prove that the rehabilitation of Dreyfus was unjust. He gently insinuated that since the law could so easily decree that yesterday's truth was today's falsehood, perhaps the attackers of General Mercier would find their relative positions reversed some day. At the same time, as a man who had always insisted that the decisions of established institutions be respected, Barrès bowed to the decision of the Court with the considerable good grace he could muster. It seemed to be Barrès' fate that he should feel called upon to protest against the actions of men in power. It was not simply that, as an unrepentant nationalist, he tended to scorn the maneuvers of opportunists. He felt most keenly any act which he thought might threaten to undercut the dignity of the Chamber and of the nation. For this reason, he voted against the proposed increase in deputies' salaries, considering that the general public would soon lose its respect for men who so blatantly sought private profit from public service. When the increase was voted anyway, he diverted his own share into the coffers of the *Ligue des Patriotes*. He at least had the satisfaction of knowing that the Republicans had unintentionally contributed to the funds of their enemies.

His decision to commit himself to the defense of the churches involved him in a scrupulous examination of conscience. He realized that he was but a lukewarm Catholic who admired the Church mainly for its history and its ceremony. Paradoxically, he believed that the Church was a valuable institution because it was not a strong one. Centuries of culture had modified it and softened it, until it contained just enough spiritualism to satisfy the ordinary religious aspirations of man, without encouraging him to fanatical extremes.[32] Any religion, he believed, consisted of a mixture of inspiration and calculation,[33] which he also named the "mystical" system and the "rational" system. The first led to mysticism, the second to dogma. If Catholicism should be displaced, he believed it would yield to a new religion with a rigid dogma and with a destructive mysticism unrestrained by centuries of development. For him, Socialism had become such a modern religion, with the added disadvantage of being resolutely internationalist in approach. All the same, Barrès hesitated before definitely making up his mind to address the Chamber. He was well aware that the outcome was decided in advance, and that his remarks would probably be interpreted as a defense of clericalism, which he in fact rejected along with any overly rigid dogma. When he finally spoke, it was to defend an integral part of French culture, without which Frenchmen were in danger of losing their national identity.[34] One point he made is particularly striking, for it shows the extent to which his writings were the fruit of long meditation. He saw that French culture revolved around two axes, symbolized by the ruins of the hill of Sion-Vaudemont and by Pasteur's laboratory.[35] The first became the subject of *La Colline inspirée*, published in 1913, the second became the hub of his postwar campaigns for massive funding of scientific research.

From 1909 onwards, Barrès found that his concerns with education were intruding more strongly into his campaign in favor of the churches. His combative spirit was aroused in January, when a teacher at the Sorbonne claimed that Joan of Arc had had no influence in winning the great French victories over the English, and cast aspersions on her relationships with the French captains. Barrès naturally had little difficulty in refuting this sort of ridiculous scandal, but he was angered that the Maid of Orleans, his compatriot and object of his admiration,[36] should have been denigrated in the eyes of impressionable students.

His concerns began to take on the appearance of a campaign when in June he questioned the minister of education concerning the suicide of a tenth-grade pupil at a lycée in Clermont-Ferrand. In his address, Barrès claimed that the suicide was proof of a serious moral deficiency in the State's lay education. He blamed agnostic professors for exciting youthful enthusiasm without providing any kind of direction. Although his remarks were moderate, their sense was clear. He accused the teachers of ridiculing nationalism and ignoring traditional French values. In passing, he criticized the tendency to name schools after famous but deplorable figures, such as Fragonard, a libertine painter, or Baudelaire, a decadent poet. Barrès' parliamentary speech received a good deal of publicity, and gave rise to a number of contradictory articles. The general argument was that the lay schools were attempting to elaborate a morality based on scientific truth, which would not be shattered by the new discoveries brought about by progress. Barrès had already evolved beyond this point of view, realizing that belief was not a question of reason, but sentiment. His detractors had attacked him on important issues, but not on the most important one of all, that the State was seemingly failing to inculcate an enthusiasm for any kind of moral system whatsoever, whether lay or religious.

Barrès' point was underscored most tragically only two months later when his own nephew, Charles Demange, committed suicide in a hotel room in Nancy. This event marked the termination of Barrès' affair with Mme de Noailles. For two years, their relations had been cool, and they had been seeing less and less of each other. Mme de Noailles had attempted to dominate Barrès, and had been embittered when he had made it clear that she was far from being the most important element in his life. On her side, the separation had been amiable in appearance only. In revenge, she set out to win Barrès' nephew. The young man was particularly susceptible in that he admired his uncle, was perhaps even a little jealous of him, and aspired to the same forms of success. Mme de Noailles reduced him to a state of dependency on her, then coldly abandoned him. Barrès never forgave her, but the damage had been done. She had destroyed Charles Demange before he had had time to free himself from his uncle's shadow or from hers, and realize the potential latent in his origins. Whatever the immediate causes, however, his death and that of the obscure schoolboy in Clermont-Ferrand were closely linked. Both had been brought too early to an awareness of the absurdity of life, without being given the time to develop a belief in any moral system which could have counteracted that absurdity.[37] Recovering from his loss, Barrès continued to protest vigorously against the bad faith of lay educators who claimed to seek truth in an impartial manner, but who failed to see that their program implied all too often the destruction of traditions and of the respect for tradition. Barrès saw repeated what had almost happened to himself in Burdeau's class thirty years before. By destroying traditional morality, the teacher also destroyed any possible respect for the lay morality which he wished to substitute. As a form of counterbalance, Barrès infused new vigor into his campaign to save the churches from collapse, and attempted also to create a focus for national morale in the person of Joan of Arc. In 1894, the senate had proposed the creation of a national holiday in her honor, but the proposition had remained tabled. Barrès now proposed that a commission be set up to bring the matter forward. The League of Patriots, with Barrès and Déroulède at its head, organized marches to her statue, and generally worked to create a favorable climate of opinion. Not all of Barrès' time was taken up with political activity, however, for *La Colline inspirée* appeared in 1913, and was integrated with his defense of the Church.

In the early months of 1914, Barrès opposed yet another scandal, this one known as the Rochette affair. At his own request, Barrès was put on a commission of enquiry into the matter, but he was in a minority. Everyone questioned was determined to know nothing. Barrès dissociated himself from the findings of the Commission, and made his own position clear in a parliamentary speech. He thought that the scandal was clear proof of the lack of direction and purpose in the body that was supposed to rule the country. The electorate made its views clear when it elected an increased number of Socialists. In Barrès' opinion, French strength and nationalism were thus further compromised by the selfish actions of political opportunists.[38]

In January, Paul Déroulède died. On 12th July, just after his return from the Middle East, Barrès was unanimously elected President of the League of Patriots, as Déroulède had hoped.

Barrès' second journey to the Middle East was far more extensive than the one he had undertaken in 1907. Its avowed purpose was to ascertain what measures could be taken to strengthen French presence in the area, and what advantages, both intangible and material, France could expect to acquire from the various peoples of the region. He returned to France at the beginning of July, rich in new experiences, and convinced that the French government would have to swallow its anti-clericalism, and give more support to the teaching orders abroad which spread French culture and created goodwill towards France. Before he could begin to put together a campaign, the First World War burst upon a troubled Europe, and Barrès diverted all his energies to maintaining a strong united France.

The German leaders had every hope of a swift French collapse. The country was in a state of political turmoil. The attempts of Barrès and the nationalists he represented, to strengthen France, had been repeatedly foiled by the pacificism and internationalism of Socialists and radicals. The Rochette affair had been but one example of the bad blood between the rival factions. On the eve of the war, Jaurès, the Socialist leader, was assassinated. There were fears that workers all over France would seek revenge, at a moment when France desperately needed unity. Although his political evolution had rapidly led him into opposition against his former sponsor, Barrès had always maintained an intense personal admiration for Jaurès. Now he wrote a letter to Jaurès' daughter expressing not only his admiration, but his sincere regret that France had lost one of her greatest leaders when he was most needed. The threatened reprisals were avoided, and France came out of the crisis with a sense of unity that had not been known for decades.

V   *In the Establishment*

Now that the events he had long prophesied had come to pass, Barrès' popularity and influence took a sudden surge,[39] increased further by the articles he was invited to write for the *Echo de Paris*. Although it is easy now to make fun of the patriotic articles Barrès churned out for the duration of the war, it should not be forgotten that he consistently did his best to maintain French unity, even when other factions were attempting to undermine it. It should not be forgotten either that the government did adopt many of the ideas he proposed for improving the lot and the morale of the civilian and military populations.

In addition to his efforts to maintain morale both in the trenches and behind the lines, Barrès played another role particularly suited to his situation as a writer. His name was as well known abroad as it was in France, so he often found himself one of the official French delegates on diplomatic or semi-diplomatic missions. In August of 1915, Barrès was invited to visit certain sections of the British army in France, including contingents from the Commonwealth. He was suitably impressed by the legendary fighting qualities of the Gurkha troops, and assured the readers of the *Echo de Paris* of the value of the British presence. In July of the following year, he visited England at the invitation of the British government. As part of the same arrangements, Rudyard Kipling toured France. Barrès visited army installations, and the steelworks at Sheffield then engaged in manufacturing armaments as fast as possible. England did not possess the same excitement as the other foreign countries he had visited. His notes mention only that the English countryside, calm and relaxing, provided a much needed rest for his nervous system.[40]

Just two months previously, he had been invited to Italy along with other French delegates, to visit Italian military installations. One of his traveling companions was Joseph Reinach, with whom Barrès had once been bitterly at odds. Accepting now the new spirit of unity, and impressed by Reinach's obvious patriotism, Barrès buried the past and thought only of France's welfare. It was in the same spirit that he lent all his support in favor of calling Clemenceau to form a government, realizing that whatever their past differences, Clemenceau was France's greatest hope for victory, and also, virtually her last.

Barrès' championship of the "Tiger" came near the climax of one of his most bitter, yet most successful political campaigns. His main target was Caillaux. That individual, audacious and power-hungry, had suffered all through the war from his exclusion from power, due to the Rochette affair. In an all-out effort to force his way into the Cabinet, he had attempted to build up a power base among those who believed that France should sue for a separate peace with Germany. For Barrès, it was clearly a case of yet another individual, cut off from his sources to spiritual culture, putting self-interest above the interest of the nation. The decision to arrest him was a bold one, for there was no real proof against him, but it was imperative that defeatism be eradicated, and that France's enemies should realize that she would not tolerate the faintest whiff of peace-mongering. Faced with an adroit mixture of political and moral charges, Caillaux went down to defeat.

There was a new political mood in France, one of determination to win at any cost. It arrived only just in time, for in 1918 came a great military crisis when German forces almost pushed through to victory, before being swept away by the Allied forces, indispensably assisted by freshly arrived American troops and materials. Barrès was highly impressed, not just with the American forces, but also with their sense of fair play and democracy. He believed that America had led the way in instituting the sort of Socialism of which he had dreamed in the 1890s, a classless society in which the progress of industrialization benefitted all equally. He looked forward after the war to close cooperation between America and Europe, and the exchange of ideas. As soon as the Armistice was signed, Barrès was in Alsace-Lorraine to play a well deserved role in the liberation ceremonies. At the beginning of December, however, he fell seriously ill, and was obliged to return to Paris.

The last five years of Barrès' life afforded him mixed blessings. He was called on more and more to give official speeches or attend official banquets, but all too often was too sick to attend, and his speeches had to be read by another person. Barrès himself was well aware that his health was precarious. He was painfully conscious of the fact that most of his family had died in their early sixties, the age he was now rapidly approaching. This foreboding, far from causing him to slow down his activity and rest, made him work all the more feverishly to ensure that France would never again be caught unprepared as in 1914. He traveled in Alsace-Lorraine and the occupied German territories on the left bank of the Rhine, conducted campaigns in favor of specific objectives which he thought would strengthen France, played an active role on the committees of which he was a member, and still found the time to write a novel ringing with a fresh, youthful lyricism.

In April of 1919, Barrès opened a campaign in the *Echo de Paris* in favor of more extensive credits for scientific research. Through timely interventions in the Chamber, he succeeded in obtaining some of the credits he asked for. His most important articles were published under the heading *Pour la haute intelligence française.*

Another of his major preoccupations was the policy France should adopt towards the conquered Rhineland states. Along with Clemenceau and other leading French figures, he believed that an attempt should be made to turn back the clock by detaching these states from Germany and setting them up as independent republics. The aim was two-fold, to create a series of buffer states between France and Germany, while using French prestige, and occupation forces if necessary to ensure that they remained within the sphere of French influence. In May and June of 1919, he made his way to Mainz to be present at the ceremonies proclaiming the Rhine republic. In the Chamber, Barrès spoke in favor of approving the Treaty of Versailles,[41] but he continued to seize every opportunity to encourage extending French influence in the Rhineland. A record of his speeches and articles on this matter was published posthumously as *Les Grands Problèmes du Rhin.* In November of 1920, Barrès was at the University of Strasbourg to present a series of five lectures on the topic of *Le Génie du Rhin.* While he was there, an American delegation from Milwaukee presented him, as president of the League of Patriots, with an American flag, a symbol of Franco-American friendship and cooperation.

The composition of the Chamber which had been returned after the war was decidedly favorable to nationalist and other right wing elements. As president of the League of Patriots, Barrès was capable of wielding a good deal of influence. This was noticeable, for example, in the adoption without discussion of his proposal for a national holiday in honor of Joan of Arc. At the beginning of 1922, in the course of a particularly stormy debate, the president of the Chamber declared that Barrès was one of those men who most honored an assembly. In addition to his leadership of the *Ligue des Patriotes,* Barrès was also president of the *Fédération des Mutilés.* In this capacity, he deployed all his talents to obtain for them the rights and privileges to which he believed they were entitled for having sacrificed themselves for France. In the Chamber, his most important official role was as vice-president of the Commission for Foreign Affairs. In this capacity, at the beginning of 1923, he was entrusted with the task of investigating the possibility of allowing the establishment of training centers in France for five missionary orders. These reports, which were accepted by the Chamber, were published posthumously as *Faut-il autoriser les Congrégations?*

Barrès' fame and authority now made him the target of sometimes importunate requests. General Lyautey, a highly competent army officer, but disregarded because he had spent most of the war years in command of his troops in Morocco, thought that he could emulate Boulanger's rise to power, and sought Barrès' support to this end. While avoiding a direct refusal, Barrès noted that Lyautey was not the man, nor was this the time for any kind of coup.[42] He had supported Clemenceau's bid for the presidential office, and was disappointed that he had not succeeded, but he saw no good reason to upset the workings of due process. In a sense, Barrès was gratified that at last there was a Chamber with which he could feel in harmony. His long years of opposition as one of the main spokesmen of a fractured minority were over. On the other hand, he was keenly aware of the dangers of his new popularity. He had always been successful in resisting enrollment in a particular group. Now, he felt himself gradually being molded and inveigled into becoming the official spokesman of his colleagues in power. He found it difficult to resist this friendly pressure, and admitted that he had been much more at ease when he had been in the opposition, and better able to maintain his independence.[43]

On 4th December 1923, Barrès presided over a meeting of the executive committee of the League of Patriots. The two main subjects of concern were the upcoming elections, and the collapse of the French-inspired Rhineland republic. At home that evening, between eleven o'clock and midnight, he was struck down by a heart attack. He died at the height of his glory, and also perhaps at the height of the influence of the ideas he stood for. A united Germany was inevitable, and not even Barrès' polemical genius could maintain the viability of an independent buffer state in the Rhineland. Although unrecognized, Hitler had thrust himself upon the scene through his abortive Munich putsch. In France, in the 1924 elections, the Left was victorious, one of the consequences being that Caillaux was rehabilitated. None of this would have mattered in the long run to Barrès. What did matter was the extent to which he had given personal expression to the innumerable elements of French civilization that had coalesced in him. Barrès had once praised Jaurès as a man of vision and a representative of humanity. At Barrès' own graveside, the same was justly said of him.

CHAPTER 2

The 'Cult of the Self'

I Sous l'oeil des Barbares

THERE is little action to be followed in this spare novel. Barrès was certainly not concerned with writing a novel of adventure, nor with writing a psychological novel after the style of Stendhal or Bourget. Consequently, there is little explanation, or even justification, of the successive states of mind described. This approach, as Barrès himself recognizes, requires a considerable effort of participation and understanding on the part of the reader. In depicting the states of mind of his young hero,[1] Barrès used symbolic figures which can lend themselves to varying interpretations. The "departure," which gives the first chapter its heading, can be understood on two levels which complement each other. Departure from the provinces to Paris is suggested, as is departure from adolescence to adulthood. Developed further, it suggests progression from dependence into self-direction. Philippe has been the victim of his teachers, who have introduced him to the most varied and contradictory ideas, and have induced in him the despair which takes over when all stimulation and excitement cease. His enthusiasm exhausted, he must try to discover by himself a way to reconcile his hopes and his skepticism.

In this first chapter, his prospects do not appear overly hopeful. His ego which was to acquire so much importance later on, had been broken up and linked with too many contradictory thinkers. Mistrustful of others, he does not yet possess the strength of character to rely solely on himself, seeking instead edification from the representatives of other philosophical systems. The only difference is that, instead of being introduced to them by teachers, he must now seek out these systems himself. Of the first two he

31

encounters, pessimism is readily definable as dedication to physical satisfaction in the absence of any positive ideal. The ass is the symbol of pessimism, denoting brutishness and stupidity which deny intellectuality and enthusiasm. Seated on the ass is the philosopher representing systemization (Système). By presenting the tableau in this fashion, Barrès intends to suggest that the way of life the philosopher outlines is based on the pessimistic denial of human values.

In view of Philippe's subsequent spiritual development, it is apparent that the philosopher's ideas, while holding little immediate appeal for him, contain a kernel of truth. The rejection of all outside attractions, as suggested by the philosopher, naturally leads to the development of the *self* as the only valid reality in the midst of an unstable, changing world. The philosopher is also mindful of the importance of freedom, and the role of material wealth in guaranteeing this freedom. His major shortcoming resides in the undue importance he gives to intellectuality. His lucidity leads him eventually to affirm that nothing new may be said about the human condition, and that no new ways can be derived to express old thoughts. In the philosopher's case, lucidity leads only to anguish, and to the desire to suppress lucidity. His encounter with the philosopher puts Philippe in a dilemma. He is strongly attracted by reason, and by the teachings of the great thinkers of the past, yet he is afraid of the unbearable sterility into which pure reason will lead him. As a result, he finds himself strongly drawn towards action, energy and heroism as a means of expressing himself. While not disdaining the variety analysis can afford, he realizes that his basic attitude must be one of enthusiasm.

When we meet Philippe in Paris, he appears to be having problems maintaining this enthusiastic attitude. Although he has recourse to sources of inspiration which have long been a focus of man's spiritual energies, such as Notre Dame cathedral, he is the victim of a rather violent reaction of sterility and discouragement. He is again in need of a new direction in which to develop, and once more, help is offered him from the outside. The major effort of the Talker (Causeur), as Barrès calls this second philosopher, is directed to bringing peace of mind to Philippe, not by revelation of any certitude, but by sketching out a day to day existence in which Philippe will have the illusion of doing something satisfactory. Philippe is encouraged to enjoy playing with illusion, and to take pleasure in the endless variety his mind can create. Paramount in the lesson is the importance attached to the value of the *self*, of which all other creations — woman, virtue, science — are but imperfect images.

Barrès parts company with the philosopher when the latter passes from the general to the particular, and outlines a specific course of action to satisfy the ambitions. It is questionable whether gratification of the ambitions would be any more satisfying than gratification of anything else to Philippe. It is essential, in any case, for him not to fall into the trap of believing in what he is doing; otherwise, Philippe realizes, he becomes one of the very barbarians he himself despises. If he does at all times maintain his awareness of the futility of ambition, then it is doubtful whether he can raise the energy to carry on. The "Causeur" proposes domination of others, because he recognizes that Philippe wants to be different and independent. After some thought, Philippe realizes that the proposition amounts to no more than that he copy the career of a Rastignac, whose main concern had been riches and renown. While he has nothing against riches, which can assure his independence, Philippe sees that to seek glory, which is no more than an opinion others have of us, would make him dependent on the approval of the very barbarians he detests. In a bitterly ironic "formula for acquiring fame with nothing" Philippe underlines the hollowness of a life dedicated to the pursuits consecrated by society. There is no use being master of your thoughts if you are not also master of your actions.

The rejection of society implied in this reasoning casts Philippe into the now familiar predicament of solitude and loneliness. As previously, however, the debits are partially balanced by some gains. He has gained some measure of self-enlightenment. He has become aware that his melancholy, far from expressing his true nature, is somewhat old-fashioned and bookish. Finally, he has glimpsed, however briefly, the possibility of modifying human values. However ironically he may treat the notion at this stage, it is an enterprise which Barrès himself, by the very act of writing, undertakes in his whole work. His avowed desire to be a teacher shows that in recounting the vicissitudes of Philippe's intellectual development, he was obeying the dictates of an ideal which, however tenuous, assumed the usefulness of his task and assured contact with others.

The effort to recapture enthusiasm explains the heading of the next chapter, "Ecstasy." The very word calls to mind Dionysian transports experienced by pagan priests when they cut themselves off from the outside world of reality to make contact with whatever higher principle permeated the universe. Unfortunately, the modern world imbues this madness with none of its former glory. Those unfortunates who are subject to it are set apart from their fellows, as of old, but none come to worship at their shrine, save Philippe. Like others of his sensitive contemporaries, frustrated in their contacts with society, Philippe envies the madman the attentive provision of physical comforts, his lack of responsibility, his power to pursue any idea which catches his fancy, without having to endure the disapproval of others. The only drawback for him lies in the madman's unawareness of his privileged situation; for Philippe considers unawareness the cardinal sin committed by the barbarian. To counter this drawback, Philippe attempts to induce within himself a lucid madness of which he remains in control at all times. His ecstasy takes the form of his embracing and being assimilated with the entire universe. It is an ideal already experienced by Flaubert's Saint Antony, and expresses the desire for perfection and for total knowledge which obsessed those writers all too sadly aware of their shortcomings. Like Saint Antony, who lived as a hermit in the desert, Philippe must experience ecstasy in solitude.

His first step in cutting off all human contacts is to depersonalize the objects of his emotions. Gradually, Philippe's concentration on ideas rather than things leads him into formulating a Cartesian view of the universe. He acknowledges a split between matter and soul, giving the latter precedence over the former. Beyond his acts, his own *self* subsists, more enduring and more real than the ephemeral actions swallowed up in a moment of time. His *self* is reflected so little in his actions, that Philippe has no compunction in disclaiming responsibility for them. His most important task is not to act consequentially, but to protect himself from the often nefarious influence of others. *Self*-preservation takes on the form of continuous creation, encouraging him to reconstruct not only his own *self,* but his whole conception of the universe in a single harmonious development.

Unfortunately, these grandiose visions are at the mercy of the slightest shock of reality, in this case a glimpse of his dirty shoes carelessly flung in a corner. The final chapter ends on a note of discouragement as Philippe, mentally and spiritually exhausted, reflects how easy it is for his inner vision to be destroyed by the outside world. The prayer which closes the book is a desperate plea to help him maintain the delicate balance between enthusiasm and skepticism, between his visions of a unified and fragmented universe, between the consolation and boredom of solitude.

In a short critical essay,[2] written soon after the publication of the last volume of the trilogy, Barrès outlined what he thought were the most important aspects of *Sous l'oeil des Barbares*. In an emphatic rejection of the common opposition between artist and non-artist, Barrès describes the barbarian as one who, consciously or unconsciously, attempts to stifle the development of another's *self*. The supposed composer of the "concordances" in which Philippe is described as others might see him, is no halfbaked materialistic Homais. He understands the shortcomings of the somewhat brutal school system, and the disappointments of a young man whose initial experiences contradict his ideals. His understanding is not, however, tempered by any sympathy. Rather like the "Causeur" this disabused barbarian believes that Philippe must fail unless he arms himself with comprehensive skepticism. As the novel progresses, the increasing brevity of the "concordances" leaves room only for a condescending comment on Philippe's actions. He shows a contempt born of misunderstanding when he derides Philippe's major axiom — develop yourself for yourself. He is consequently unable to imagine Philippe's split between his actions and his thoughts, and cannot believe that Philippe's actions leave Philippe indifferent. Finally, in exasperation, the barbarian brands Philippe as a contradictory, illogical person who suffers from unhappiness while also judging happiness to be a state fit only for the mediocre. It is quite true that Philippe's aspirations appear at times to be contradictory. There is unity, however, in his abiding desire to achieve development through the cultivation of fresh sensation.

With the benefit of hindsight, the modern critic can see that Barrès' demonstration of the development of the *self* as the assimilation of fresh impressions, closely parallels Bergson's description in *Time and Free Will*.[3] In this first novel, Barrès affirms the importance of protecting the *self* against hostile elements, while developing it by assimilation of harmonious elements. Although he does not minimize the importance of reason, Barrès believes that the fresh sensations which aid the development of the *self,* must first be recognized intuitively. He claims that his first novel is an account of Philippe's struggle to understand his own *self,* and to reject the foreign teaching which has overlaid it.

The difficulty of the struggle is most readily seen in the symbol of Woman, perhaps the most complex and contradictory of the puppet figures Barrès created as vehicles for some of his ideas. He made it quite clear that he was not interested in people or events themselves, but in the traces they leave upon the mind of his principal character. The woman he describes does not exist in her own right, but as an object created to highlight certain aspects of Philippe's nature.

In the first chapter, the young woman presents in embryonic form some of the most important notions to which Philippe will later subscribe, but which at this early stage, he fails to recognize. She suggests that he seek wisdom, not from the philosophy of others, but in himself. At the same time, she attempts to dissuade him from isolating himself from the rest of the universe — in this respect, she is a predecessor of Bérénice. At the end of the chapter, she represents intuition, as opposed to the sterile reason of philosophy, when she echoes Rabelais' advice to seek intoxication. At this stage, however, Woman embodies for Philippe a sort of animal instinct of which he is contemptuous. Whether consciously or not, he is still influenced by Baudelaire's axiom that Woman is natural, therefore abominable. He is also too much influenced by Schopenhauer's view of Woman as a rather ignorant creature, too obsessed with the physical to respond to man's spiritual aspirations. For this reason, Philippe is discouraged from attempting to turn her into the sort of ideal companion he would like to participate in the development of his self. By her failure to be a companion, the Woman turns into an enemy bent on preventing man from reaching his spiritual goal.

In the first two chapters, then, the role of Woman becomes all the more clearly defined in Philippe's mind. Initially a possible ally, she swiftly changes into a definite antagonist. From this point on, there can be little communication between them. When next he encounters her, she has lost her fresh innocence of youth, and put on the frivolous mask of the flirt. By liberating himself from the influence of woman, Philippe intends to liberate himself from that part of his soul preoccupied with vulgar ambition and mean preoccupations. Woman finds grace in his eyes when she is virginal in body and spirit, isolating herself from a barbaric society she disdains. On one level, Philippe echoes the view of his contemporaries. Virginity and accompanying sterility deny woman's natural role, thereby rescuing her from being abominable while neutralizing the major weapon with which she brings man down to the level of mundane reality. On another level, however, Philippe's rejection of Woman, envisaged as a rejection of part of his self, represents a failure to develop himself totally. In this respect, Philippe is far from prefiguring Bergsonism. Indeed, one of his major tasks will be to learn to accept the more deplorable parts of his nature, just because they are part of himself.

The flight into the past, which occupies the whole of the third chapter, is a minor episode, but one nevertheless worthy of more than passing note. A retreat to the past was in this period a device used frequently by authors who detested the society in which they were forced to live and work. A case in point is Huysmans' hero, Durtal, who was a sick man until he undertook a therapeutic investigation into the life and times of Gilles de Rais. Such is not the case with Barrès, who describes the decline of Hellenism — when barbaric hordes stifled the last representatives of a superior culture — not to escape into a period more congenial than his own, but to objectify his aspirations so as to recognize them more clearly. He was too much the champion of lucidity to hide his head in the sand. The past he describes parallels the present, revealing, rather than obscuring it. It is with the firm determination to keep his eyes open, and not retreat into illusion, that Barrès sets about his second novel.

II Un Homme libre

Philippe has found a companion whose presence facilitates that analysis which alone can augment the pleasure of exaltation. He is eager to forge a new life with the twin tools of reason and ardor. Ardor is reflected particularly in the obtrusive religious vocabulary. It may be found in the chapter headings (In a state of Grace; The militant Church; the triumphant Church) and also in Philippe's musings on the style of life he might have liked to lead. According to him, his ideal of exaltation augmented by analysis would be most readily met by a strict monastic order. In *Sous l'oeil des Barbares,*

Philippe envied the liberty of the madman in the asylum. The monk enjoys the same sort of liberty as the madman, with the added advantage of lucidity. It is probably as well that Philippe did not take the step of trying out the monastic life. Although he uses religious vocabulary, although he aspires to a religious fervor, his goal is not to seek God. He is motivated, not by love of another being, but by egoism. His major task is to learn to understand himself in the hope that comprehension will lead to control. Religious and military vocabulary blend as he expresses his admiration and enthusiasm for Loyola's spiritual exercises which, he believes, will lead him to the same mastery over the movements of his soul that a captain has over the movements of his troops.

Although Philippe disdains the actions his body performs, and refuses to see in them any significance for his spiritual development, he is unclear to what extent he should make the split between body and mind. Living in an age of positivism and materialism, he cannot help being impressed by those philosophers and scientists who see in mental and physical phenomena basically similar patterns of action and reaction governed by ultimately comprehensible laws. The majority of his scattered comments tend to support the view that mind and body interact upon each other equally. He aims to maintain himself in a permanent state of enthusiasm and exaltation by understanding the laws governing the secretion of enthusiasm. Like Zola, Philippe believes that when you understand a mechanism, you can successfully control it to your own advantage by intervention. Understanding the human mechanism threatens, however, to prove an arduous and interminable task. More rapid success is promised by the substitution of one's own laws artificially created by habit. Taking as his guide the rules of the more austere monastic orders, Philippe sets up rules of silence, spiritual meditation and physical exercise. They do not have as their aim the glorification of God, but are intended as spiritual corsets to stiffen his enthusiasm. He develops in addition a mnemonic technique, adapted from Loyola's spiritual exercises, which enables him to recall a given emotion at will. It consists of linking a deep emotion with some material object. Recollection of the object will in turn recreate the emotion.

By the development of mechanical habit, Philippe attempts to apply the first part of his program, the creation of a state of exaltation. His next step must be to multiply the forms of this exaltation through analysis and contemplation. Since this stage of the program will be undertaken by his intellect, it is important that he discover where its strengths and weaknesses lie. He discerns three sorts of weaknesses, or sin, by thought, word and deed in descending order. Sin by thought is the worst, because man is fashioned by what he thinks. He also blames himself for sin by word when he has accidentally allowed himself to be influenced by something he has said. For Philippe, sin is anything which prevents self-expansion. Sin by deed therefore has little importance, since his actions mean so little to him.

The point of this examination is to prevent him from falling into the traps he has previously failed to avoid. At this stage in his evolution, Philippe has succeeded in envisaging the sort of life he would like to lead. He has emphatically rejected all the propositions made to him in *Sous l'oeil des Barbares,* and now knows the methods he will employ to achieve his aim. His difficulty still lies in ensuring that these methods are the correct ones. If they are not, they will not work, but he can only find out whether or not they will work by putting them to the test. As a result, Philippe continues in his customary pattern of trial and error. The success his methods enjoy teaches him something about himself; but he also seeks to discover more about himself by other means, so as to ensure the greater success of the methods he chooses in the future. From this point, the novel takes up once again the quest first undertaken in *Sous l'oeil des Barbares* to understand the self.

As a first step, Philippe uses famous figures whom he calls mediators (intercesseurs). These are people he admires because he believes they come close to incarnating the ideal he wishes to create for himself. Barrès had used the same technique four years previously,[4] but then his choice of mediator had been Baudelaire. Now, having passed beyond the point where Baudelaire can be useful to him, he chooses Benjamin Constant and the youthful Sainte-Beuve. They promote self-knowledge by giving Philippe greater awareness of something in his own nature which was previously obscure. Their role is limited, however, to this and little else. Their usefulness is soon exhausted, and Philippe must accept the fact that they cannot give him total revelation of his own *self*. Their similarities are fragmentary, and if he tries to mold himself on their total personality, they become foreign influences harmful to his spiritual development. But even this disappointment is not devoid of usefulness. Philippe has learned that there are parts of himself which cannot be revealed by mediators, and that he must turn to other sources to expose them. He believes that in a sense, he is working backwards. Individual mediators can show him the inner meaning of the most recent developments of his *self* which take place after his introduction to literature and philosophy. The more obscure forces which exert influence in his earlier formative years cannot be uncovered by meditating upon individuals.

As a result, Philippe resolves to pass from reflection on the individual to reflection on the group. He will consider his own history as a succinct history of his birthplace, Lorraine. There are two movements in Philippe's meditation, the first of despair, the second of hope. In the first, he sees a Lorraine which has failed to develop its potential, and which can now only disintegrate and furnish sustenance to future mutations. In the second, Philippe realizes that far from having to mold his development to the history of Lorraine, he is himself a favorable mutation, a typical product of Lorraine, but with the leisure to develop himself in an open minded way, free from the pressure of events. It has been pointed out[5] that there is no guarantee that Philippe and Lorraine can revivify each other, and that they might just as easily devitalize each other. This argument ignores Philippe's belief that inner strength comes from an understanding of the self. Lorraine will help him to know himself, and he in turn will teach Lorraine her role in a changing society. We have here the first step in the development of Barrès' belief that Lorraine must act as a filter to protect France from Eastern influence.

The meditation on Lorraine gives way to part 3 — "the Church Triumphant." Despite this heading, the first chapter continues the mixed hope and despair of the preceding one. The pessimistic tone stems from Philippe's knowledge that he must destroy the way of life he has established with Simon, while he is still uncertain of what the future holds. Yet the change is necessary if he is to put into practice that flash of insight afforded him in Lorraine. The presence of Simon has helped him examine the past and disentangle the events which had led up to the formation of his self. Now, Lorraine has taught him not to spend too much time in contemplation of the past. It is time for Philippe to imagine the ideal he would like to become, and work towards it, developing his own potential and that of Lorraine of which he is part. Simon cannot aid him in this enterprise. Two people cannot guess what the future will be through discussion, so they will have to separate and meditate. Philippe's meditation will take the form of an enthusiastic patterning on the example of a mediator. This mediator will not be an individual, nor will it be Lorraine. He has extracted from Lorraine what he can and must now look for a group more closely representing the ideal he would like to realize within himself.

He does not explain why he elected to go to Venice. The choice is an instinctive one based on the dry facts of a Baedecker guide. Philippe feels that he will discover what he is seeking, and he naturally does so because he closes his mind to anything else. The point is underscored by the anecdote of the young man who blindly admires a painting which everyone elses knows not to be a da Vinci. What does it matter, Philippe asks, that his admiration is based on a falsehood? It is more important to have ardor than common sense. Enthusiasm and self-development are often cramped by the search for objective truth which, because it is exteriorized, may often be different from the inner truth of the *self*. It is much more appropriate to turn your gaze, not outwards, but inwards, and try to accept all aspects of one's personality. Now that he is ready to accept this lesson, Philippe finds it in da Vinci's portrait of Christ, a Christ who accepted everything, even his own destiny and the mediocrity of his followers. Acceptance in this sense is understanding, sympathy and even indulgence. Philippe has progressed since the time he refused to cultivate certain aspects of his personality because he was repelled by them and afraid of the forces their cultivation would unleash. Now, if anything in his personality strikes him as disorderly, he attempts to see it simply as an incomplete manifestation of future perfection.

This method should also lead him to the unity he has long sought. Acceptance is combinative, systemizing scattered and disjointed emotions. Analysis, adjunct of reason and major tool of those who wish to bring their intelligence to bear on exterior reality, is divisive. The hostility of external reality makes it important that Philippe adopt a careful attitude toward Venice. It should not be allowed to overcome him and swamp his personality. Philippe must react with Venice and adapt it to his own nature. This is why his most fruitful encounter with Venice takes place in the isolation of his room, where he can unite his scattered impressions into a single idea. The notion he develops is clearly a product of his own personality, not an objective view of Venice.[6]

The importance of his visit is to convince him of the truth of the maxim he outlines in the dedication, "The only solution I propose is continually to seek peace and happiness with the conviction that they will never be found."[7] It is difficult to seek perfection knowing that it can never be attained. Philippe had previously tried to do this by concentrating his attention not on his goal, but on his actions. On the rare occasions he imagines he has attained the perfection he seeks, it appears to him as a feeling of plenitude and satisfaction.

Naturally, these moments are fleeting. Perfection lasts only as long as one is not aware of it. The contemplation of perfection implies a split which allows part of the mind to contemplate itself, and this very split destroys unity. One can only enjoy the experience of perfection when it is past, and when the critical faculties have been reawakened. Philippe remains in a state of alternation between the better and the best. Venice has been a moment of perfection, but it can now offer nothing new and must remain just a pleasant memory. All that cannot be absorbed into his personality must necessarily disappear, lest it become an obstacle to further development. He must seek stimulation from new sources. It is for this reason that he returns to Parisian society.

Although Philippe does not make a clear distinction between the irrational and the suprarational, he seems to be groping toward a definition that would distinguish between the two in Bergsonian terms. The irrational is natural instinct, appealing to man's lowest passions and basest desires. The man who gives way to them yields himself to an unknown force which Philippe assumes is antagonistic to his welfare. The determination to stifle one's instinctive movements might be attributed to Schopenhauer's mistrust of nature and the desire to trick her; but Philippe's ambition seems more positive than this. While distrusting instinct, he praises intuition which alone can enable him to grasp the secret of his inner development, and avoid succumbing to outside influences. This intuition, although transcending analysis, is based firmly on it.

His choice made, Philippe will impose meaning on the outside world through an act of will, and through imagination and memory he will recreate pleasure. The excitement he has known has made him more sensitive, and has enriched his being in general. It has also taught him the necessity of asserting his own self at all times, so as to turn it into a sanctuary which will remain inviolate. Although he insists so strongly upon the importance of his inner self, his desire for unity, which had often accompanied it, is modified. He realizes that unity cannot be achieved by restriction, but rather through development of an evolving multifaceted personality. He now intends to allow the numerous parts of his self to evolve as they will, while imposing unity on them through will and contemplation. He reaches back in time to affirm the teaching of his Jesuit instructors that acts do not necessarily represent the soul behind them, and may be interpreted in any number of ways.

As a result, Philippe loses his fear of the outside world, which he sees as less perilous than the two extremes of sterility and over-enthusiasm within himself. He also loses his fear of the barbarians, and comes to accept them. While continuing to refuse to be part of society, he will move within it, aware now that it cannot touch him. Barrès uses the term "outsider" in much the same way as Camus does to designate his free man who is *in* the world, but not *of* it. Like Meursault, Philippe cannot see any special meaning in life, only perpetual movement towards no particular end. He consoles himself, and even feels joy, not in sensual pleasure as Meursault, but in intellectual pleasure, stimulated from time to time by carefully controlled excursions into novelty. These conclusions are by no means new, but are scattered throughout the two novels. But by this time, Philippe has tested, refined, and transcended intellectual acceptance of them to incorporate them as part of his evolving self. He realizes that he has at last attained a higher state, a sort of plateau, which can be used as a base for future progress.

III   Le Jardin de Bérénice

In this last novel of the trilogy, Philippe finds himself in the Camargue, seeking election to Parliament as a Boulangist candidate. As such, he must make an appeal to the masses, which differentiates him from such as Flaubert or Huysmans, who held the people in abhorrence. Critics have stated that Barrès was illogical, because he turned for support to the very Barbarians he originally despised.[8] This is not quite fair. The barbarian is Charles Martin, the educated man who has substituted reason for sympathy. Philippe has transcended this attitude and seeks now the intuition of the creative urge inhabiting the deepest recesses of the inarticulate masses. As is frequent with Philippe, his quest takes the form of an imagined conversation. It is in imagined conversation with the spirit of Lorraine that Philippe reaches his decision to probe his future development instead of his past. At the end of this novel, Philippe acquires fresh insight in conversation with the spirit of Bérénice. These ethereal spirits apparently have little in common with Renan and Chincholle, the two corporeal participants in the discussion which opens the first chapter. Both of them, however, like Lorraine and Bérénice, represent different aspects of Philippe's self. Renan is that curiosity and spirit of enquiry which encourage Philippe to study himself, while Chincholle is that energy which pushes him into action.

It is fitting that these two apparently contradictory forces should combine in Philippe; Renan's theory of knowledge inciting him to adopt Chincholle's political stance. Through Renan, Philippe formulates a claim to which his theories of the group have been logically leading him — that a nation is represented by the mass of its subjects. Philippe's political notions are curiously similar to those of another seeker after his *self,* Jean-Jacques Rousseau. The idea that the nation as an entity is something greater than the masses which make it up is akin to Rousseau's claim that the General Will is greater than the sum of individual wills of which it is composed. It is fitting, then, that on the following page, Barrès should intone a song of praise to Rousseau.[9] The nation, when it represents the people working together harmoniously and instinctively, is infallible.

Unfortunately, it is impossible to know until after the event whether or not the nation represents the masses as a whole, or merely a few individual wills who have illegitimately seized control. To understand what the hidden aspirations of the masses are, Philippe attempts to become part of them through emotion and instinct while standing apart from them through the exercise of his lucidity. He attempts to recreate the masses' past and present, as he had done for himself, so that he can project their future. His final comments show Philippe in the role of teacher. He wishes to lead the inarticulate individuals who make up the masses to a higher awareness of their own selves. Philippe claims that every man is a repository of the common soul without being aware of it. This soul can emerge in the atmosphere of the political meeting, where the excitement makes a man forget his own particular self and his own particular interests. Barrès hopes that by attaining this state the masses can avoid the pitfall of blind subservience to alien ideas which characterizes the barbarians.

Philippe's attachment to the people is the result of his quest for the meaning of his own self. He had progressed from study of himself as an isolated individual, through study of himself as part of a group, to study of himself as part of humanity. Helping the people develop self-awareness is part of the task of increasing his own self-awareness and projecting himself towards the goal of unity which has been his abiding aim. At one stage, this aim takes the form of a desire for immortality through association with something stable and permanent. It is not personal immortality he seeks. He has long realized that the parts of his self will eventually be dissolved and re-assembled to form a richer unit. His immortality will consist in the part he has played as a lucid representative of the collective consciousness, to raise it to a higher level. His confidence in the people is really confidence in himself and in the validity of his self-imposed task.

Despite frequent expressions of confidence, Philippe's development is hampered by confusion in the way he describes his progress towards a higher expression of his self. When he considers the changes he has undergone, he is tempted to describe his life as an eternal succession of destruction and creation. In this respect, Barrès anticipates Sartre's notion that the present is built on the ruin of the past, and that the creation of a new self entails the destruction of the old one. Such a notion is disastrous for Philippe's conception of unity in total perfection. It implies that it will always be impossible to be anything other than fragmentary. It may be possible to have many experiences in the course of a lifetime, but one would be aware of only one or two at a time. Such a vision of the world affords a clear notion of the perpetual transformation of the universe — without any awareness of the total unity towards which it is hopefully progressing.

As an alternative to the theory of perpetual destruction and creation of the *self*, the notion of *continuity* is offered. This is a particularly Bergsonian notion which assures the conservation of past characteristics in a constantly changing harmony. *Continuity* is suggested to Philippe from many different sources. The country-side around Aigues-Mortes, and Bérénice herself show him how old values can repeat themselves in new patterns. In Philippe's elaboration of the notion of *continuity,* Charles Martin, the Paris trained engineer is valuable as an irritant. It is in opposition to him that Philippe clarifies some of his most important ideas. He criticizes Martin for his blind, complacent rationalism, and for seeking to impose changes on the topology of the region which, while sound from an engineering point of view, are not in harmony with the spirit of the land and its people. Charles Martin and Bérénice form two opposites. The former stands apart from the subject he studies and refuses to enter into communication on any other than a rational plane. Bérénice is instinctive and spontaneous, fusing herself completely with her surroundings.

Philippe, while he obviously prefers Bérénice, does not give complete approval to one or the other. If Charles Martin is reason without sympathy, Bérénice is sympathy without reason. Both are incomplete. Bérénice passively represents the soul of the land without realizing its tremendous potentiality and diversity. Charles Martin sees its superficial diversity without grasping its underlying unity. Philippe wants to combine the best attributes of the two, so that they eventually appear as stages which he has surpassed in his own development.

The method Philippe outlines through comparison of these two individuals is outstandingly Bergsonian. Bergson respected science, believing it to be a useful tool for the investigation of the self. He criticized science only when it excluded everything else. He was equally critical of instinct unilluminated by the light of reason, preferring to speak of intuition and suprarationality rather than of instinct and irrationality. Philippe anticipates some of the future developments of Bergsonism. He even uses the term "creative energy"[10] when he is speaking of the aspirations of the masses. By this, he means that the masses have an obscure notion of their destiny, and attempt to become this destiny. Evolution is not a matter of chance, but is the response of an organism attempting to fulfill its innermost being.[11] The key to progress is recognition of one's own insufficiency, and the consequent desire to develop. Both Bergson and Philippe grant man a vague intuition of his own perfection which maintains his development along purposeful lines.

While Philippe is sure that this motion towards perfection exists, he is not always successful in his efforts to make himself aware of it. His most striking failure occurs when he attempts to reform some superficial lesbian tendencies on the part of Bérénice. It is not easy to understand why he should have been so shocked when he had finally wrung a confession from her lips. His reaction duplicates the horrified reaction of the Barbarian whom he despises, and blinds him to the fact that Bérénice is unconsciously putting into practice one of his own favorite axioms — the separation between acts and sentiments is desirable. Her relationship with Bougie-Rose is nothing more than a convenient means of maintaining pure and intact the memory of her dead lover. Philippe understands nothing of this and, with visions of debauched experimentation in mind, peevishly accuses her of contradicting her natural instincts. Nothing could be further from the truth. It is Philippe himself who lends too much weight to accepted ideas, a deplorable lapse on the part of a would-be free man.

Thinking only of the necessity of enabling her to satisfy her animal desires in a more conventional manner, Philippe hustles her into marriage with Charles Martin. It matters little that he knows the two to be incompatible; rather, he hopes that their incompatibility will make Bérénice regress to the stage of being an unconscious representative of the racial instinct. The experiment fails dismally. Bérénice is too refined to regress to pure animality. Development, as Philippe is well aware, is one-way only; forward, not backward. The lesson is that if it is difficult to understand yourself, it is even more difficult to understand others. As he watches by Bérénice's deathbed, he realizes that he has misinterpreted the unconscious motivation of her development. He has not tried to understand and conform to her inner self, but has instead treated her as an object to be manipulated and changed at will. The experience has repercussions on his political attitude. If he cannot understand Bérénice, how can he claim to understand the people? He finally decides that his strong sympathy notwithstanding, the most he can do is to work for the creation of a climate conducive to the development of the people's self-awareness. He cannot intervene directly in their evolution, but only watch it.

By limiting his action to the creation of favorable circumstances, Philippe resolves a further dilemma posed in an imaginary conversation between Seneca and Lazarus. Seneca represents an attitude Philippe once held but which he has now outstripped. He is the dilettante who cultivates every sensation for its own sake in an attempt to enlarge his own self. Because he considers himself an individual isolated from the rest of humanity, his development, deprived of any guiding force is fragmentary. Lazarus represents the possibility of action in the form of fanaticism. Like Philippe, he is inhibited by the knowledge that his actions are not underpinned by any demonstrable certitudes. The fanatic acts directly upon men. By restricting himself to providing men with the opportunity to develop themselves, Philippe avoids the pitfalls of direct action while giving himself the satisfaction of carrying out a useful task — not forgetting his determination to be himself and develop his own personality.

Taken as a whole, the trilogy mirrors Barrès' attempts to assert his own personality in the face of established schools of thought. His determination to seek novelty often enabled him to avoid temptations which might otherwise have ensnared him. He was in many ways attracted by the Romantic example of the superior artist; but he recognized also the sterility of the artist who excludes himself from society. His strong streak of sadism is reminiscent of the dandy; yet if he is severely critical of dandyism it is because he has discerned the severe limits put on the dandy's scope of action.

The influence of Naturalism is perhaps slight, but there are some intriguing parallels. Philippe seems to accept the connection between mental attitudes and physical condition. He even speaks of one day discovering a law which will operate like a chemical reaction and enable him unerringly to reproduce the same mental reaction each time he operates. This is something more than the psychology of Pascal or Loyola which relies on habit and mechanical repetition to bend the mind to a particular pattern of thought. They teach that mental concentration, reinforced by habit, is stronger than the temptation of the physical world. Barrès, implicitly recognizing the strength of the physical world, seeks to use its laws to favor his spiritual development, or at the very least, avoid contradicting it. A further link with Naturalism, curious in the light of Barrès' complete indifference to public opinion, is his effort to prove that his work has something of the value of a document for the social historian. Like Zola, whose wish to promote a point of view while retaining the objectivity of science led him to formulate a theory of "moral impersonality," Barrès adopts a distinction between didacticism and teaching. While not overtly one-sided, his works do tend to a definite point of view. He does not force people to adopt his viewpoint, but he does everything to assure them that they will be better off to adopt it. Finally, Barrès shows superficial links with Naturalism in that both he and Zola demonstrate concern for the welfare of the masses. Naturalism concentrates principally on their material welfare. At least in his actions as a politician, Barrès thought of their material well-being; but in his novels he is much more concerned with their spiritual development. This concern, at just the beginning of its development in *Le Jardin de Bérénice,* acquires a greater importance in the next stage of Barrès' career.

CHAPTER 3

The 'Cult of the Self' Prolonged

BETWEEN the period of the cult of the ego and the period of nationalism whose opening is signalled by *Les Déracinés,* there is a period during which Barrès sought to portray himself as a representative of humanity and also as a leader. One of his first tasks was to affirm the differences between himself and those leaders of an earlier generation who had most influenced him. Consequently, his first attacks are against two giants, Renan and Taine.[1]

His disappointment with Renan stems from the contrast between the strength of Renan's ideas and the timidity of his person. In his desire for peace, Renan had refrained from using his authority to support moral or social judgments. All that Barrès says of Renan portrays him as too self-satisfied, too immersed in study to ask himself the question, "Have I been able to take advantage of all the opportunities offered by circumstances to ennoble my being?"[2] This question, which Philippe might well have asked himself, shows the extent to which Barrès still acts according to the ideas of the *Cult of Self.*

If Barrès gradually grew disenchanted with the person of Renan, his attachment to Taine, and particularly to Taine's method, increased with time. Taine's fortunes had undergone a curious reversal. Criticized as revolutionary when it first appeared, his work towards the end of his life was attacked for being reactionary. Ignoring Taine's conclusions which had given rise to these judgments, Barrès claimed that the true value of the work lay in the method he had elaborated. This method consisted of teaching how to see clearly, so that it would be possible to understand the reasons behind everything that happens. All his courage and independence resided in the defense of his method as a means of analysis and understanding. If Barrès occasionally criticized some of Taine's

50

affirmations, he always claimed to criticize them from the point of view of the method he ascribed to Taine himself.

I   Toute Licence sauf contre l'amour

This slim work aims at rallying all uncommitted students. The structure Barrès uses is based on Hegel's dialectical method, although he is as familiar with Hegel's philosophy as any cultivated man who prefers to glean his knowledge from popular vulgarizations. He takes as his thesis the notion of action. In his introduction, he claims that action is the desire to influence the events of the real world. He believes that students, far from committing themselves totally to action, are using student organizations as a means of sheltering themselves from the outside world while maintaining a relatively secure position. Unwittingly, they are regimented. Already the victims of a centralized education, they sink into a gray, uniform mass. They accept mediocre men as their leaders. One can only hope that the superior man will cut himself loose and develop his own personality in isolation.

The antithesis shows that if the superior man succeeds in escaping from the clutches of his mediocre fellows by putting into practice the clairvoyance of Taine's method, he runs the risk of falling into skepticism. When he speaks of the skeptic, Barrès does not intend to designate Bourget's skeptic who has toyed with all manner of philosophical notions without adopting any of them seriously. Nor is the skeptic the semicultured man who adopts other people's opinions as his own. He is the man who, contemptuous of ordinary, banal, everyday things, seeks to broaden his knowledge and develop his own self. He is Philippe of *Un Homme libre*. The skeptic's main problem is that he always tends to see too many sides of a question at once. He runs the danger of becoming another Renan, contemptuous of those around him and defending his own personal tranquility against them. In such a situation most opportunities for effective action are lost.

The third chapter, the synthesis, discusses the problems of reconciling thought and action. There is no lack of problems to be solved — the strengthening of the French nation; the bonding of the old France and the democratic France; the reconciliation of labor and capital; the elaboration of new social theories to conform with the latest scientific ideas. How are these problems to be resolved by a man who sees too many solutions to accept any one of them? Are thinkers sterile, at least as far as practical life is concerned? A person who joins a political party has to become partisan and adopt some views in which he does not believe. If he steps outside all parties, as Boulanger attempted to do, he eventually creates a disparate one of his own which engages him willy-nilly in a program not well adapted to his personality. Outside of politics, writers and teachers face the problem of responsibility, for few others are capable of understanding them properly. In view of all these problems, Barrès' solution is disarmingly simple. He proclaims that the only rule should be to love; the only restriction should be against hurting others; and the only sure method is the cult of the personality. His solution is valid only if one is primarily concerned with development of the personality, because the desire to love in no way guarantees that one will not hurt others. Too many questions are left in the air with no solution at all.

II   L'Ennemi des lois

This novel expands the main theme of *Toute Licence sauf contre l'amour*. When he has to express his ideas in bare arguments, Barrès is undeniably weak. Primarily a master of evocation, he experienced the need to create characters who would flesh out his theories. Barrès was able to operate the same sleight of hand as the Naturalist novelist. While claiming that his characters' development illustrates the validity of his theories, he is the one who secretly manipulates them so that they conform to his ideas.

The first person to be presented is a young professor, André Maltère, on trial for incitement to riot because he happened to print some rather unflattering comments concerning the army. André's conduct is almost too good to be true. The limpid clarity of his arguments makes his accusers appear rather ridiculous. By his complete detachment he distinguishes himself from all others and their banal concerns. He appeals to the small elite that Barrès admired, and to bored society women — for whom Barrès felt contempt — but whom he was quite prepared to dazzle. Remembering the scorn that Barrès is to heap on the intellectuals at the time of Dreyfus' trial, and his impassioned defense of the army and national honor, it is comic to see him here taking the side of the intellectuals against the defenders of order. The credo André Maltère lives by is already familiar. He strives to maintain his individual freedom in order to think clearly and communicate his thoughts for the good of humanity. At the outset of the novel he is, however, in a dilemma. He is aware of what ought to be changed, but he is not at all clear what it should be changed to. He is sure only of his own desires.

While waiting to begin his prison sentence, André makes contact with two women of quite different temperaments. Claire, the daughter of a prominent scientist, has inherited her father's intellectual spirit and rational approach. She is rich and wants to help others but does not know how. André tries to tell her that if everyone rejects that part of society which causes him pain then society will be transformed. It is a question not of forcing men to adapt to society, but of adapting society to the taste of each individual. Maltère does not seem to take into account the possibility that individuals, being different, will attempt to call forth contradictory forms of society. Claire is too ill-assured to accept this blind confidence in the future. André is obliged to educate her slowly, by describing how society has come to be what it is, before trying to guess how it should develop in the future. Together they undertake a study of Saint-Simon, one of the major theorists of collectivism before Fourier, Proudhon or Marx. With the advantage of hindsight, Maltère can easily put his finger on Saint-Simon's insights and weaknesses. Saint-Simon's strength has been his combination of a call for social reform with religious zeal. People are influenced to greater extent by an appeal to faith, rather than to reason. His major shortcoming stems from his exclusive interest in economic reform. Industrialized society had progressed out of the control of its creators, owing to a lack of concern over how it might influence human nature.

As can be expected from what we know of Barrès' penchant for Proudhon,[4] Maltère inclines more to Fourier, who concerned himself, not with materialistic theories, but with man, particularly how to use human nature for the good of society as a whole. Modern critics, with the advantage of longer hindsight than Barrès, know that Fourier was far from being the answer to the social dilemma. Even Barrès, after a passing fancy, lost all interest in him. The value of André Maltère's interest in Fourier is as an illustration of Barrès' concern, not with ideas or social institutions, but with temperaments. None of this answers directly Claire's question about what to do to improve the human lot. It does, however, put her on her guard, and warn her that in the absence of deep-rooted sympathy and understanding, attempts to impose values from above will likely turn out badly.

In contrast to Claire, rational but slow to sympathize, Marina is quick and intuitive. This Russian princess is of the same family as Astiné Arévian. Barrès' attitude towards the personality of Marina was gradually modified as the significance of her role in the novel became clearer to him. In his first rough sketches for this character she had appeared to him to be the incarnation of selfishness and evil.[3] In *L'Ennemi des lois* she is used as an object lesson. Her selfishness and amorality remain, but are compensated for by perfect good taste. She is flippant and sensuous, but possesses an intuitive understanding of people. Claire is interested in André for his ideas, but Marina is interested in him as an individual. Together, the two women pose André Maltère a problem of which he has hereto remained unaware. As part of his humanitarian ideal, he is committed to the reconciliation of widely diverse types. Claire is the rationalism of France; Marina is the mysterious unknown of orientalism. André attempts to fuse these two contradictory forces in his own personality, but succeeds only in vacillating between them. Before his marriage to Claire he visits Venice with Marina, seeking principally the sensuality and refinement of its beauty. With Claire in Germany he studies German thinkers, Marx in particular.

Although his attitude towards Germany and the Germans is less bellicose at this early stage in his career, Barrès views them in much the same light that he does later on. Maltère views their main trait as materialism and insistence on physical well-being. He pays particular attention to their capacity for food and drink which he regards, not unkindly, as a salutary manifestation of instinctive animality, if not an all-important consideration.

There is some similarity in the attitude towards the Jews. Under a veneer of indulgence are critical views which will be intensified with Barrès' later intransigence. Jews, he says, are cold-blooded and logical. They see human affairs as an interplay of impersonal forces which they can calculate with mathematical precision.[4] Thanks to Marina and her example of the importance of sensuality, André Maltère has become aware of the need to express love for mankind. Thanks to her basic good taste, he has learned to trust in the unconscious desires of the people. He can express confidence in the notion — close to Bergsonian creative evolution — that once any theoretical idea is integrated into the needs and desires of the people it comes to fruition, as an apple tree bears an apple. He rejects, then, all idea of social reform. Even humanitarianism, if imposed from above, can be totalitarianism. Instead, he resolves to sensitize the masses, to create a state of mind which includes the need to be happy. Claire and André decide that their goal must be to communicate their enthusiasm and passion to others.

By the standards of Barrès, who tends to subordinate exciting plot to hairsplitting theoretical discussion, the novel ends dramatically; although looked at dispassionately, the dilemma is resolved in the traditional triangular situation of the typical French bedroom farce. Recognizing André's obvious longing for Marina, Claire encourages him to gratify his need without remorse. The three of them are then united by a solid bond through their shared efforts to save a pet dog from the cruel hands of a vivisectionist. All three decide to return to the country and found a college for the education of others.

The meaning of the title, *The Enemy of Laws,* becomes clear in this final chapter. André, like Auguste Comte, believes that humanity goes through a process of evolution from one stage to another. In the early stages, man needs the framework of laws to support him, but they become unnecessary as he progresses in intelligence and sensitivity. The account of Marina's life teaches how a selfish young girl, who has often set out to hurt others deliberately, is sensitized by suffering and becomes more considerate. Claire rises above accepted laws and morality when she encourages Marina to share her life and André's. It is in this evolutionary context that we should regard the often quoted complaint in the introduction, "The dead stifle us."[5] Barrès attacks the dead when they are mummified in the rigid forms of the past. When they are incorporated in an evolving system, Barrès can then accept the dead and the traditions they stand for.

Barrès intends to give a practical example of the conclusion he reaches in *Toute licence sauf contre l'amour* but on reflection, it can be seen that he has done little more than recreate Rabelais' *Abbaye de Thélème.* This insistence on love and good taste, rather than on laws is a modern version of "Fais ce que vouldras." The comparison points up some dangers in Barrès' more ambitious scheme. Rabelais limits membership in his *Abbaye* to people of high breeding. Barrès undertakes to educate the masses and raise them to a higher level of sensitivity. His proposal to set up a school in the country where the pupils will derive their lessons from the example of nature is a strongly Rousseauistic one, recalling the desire for simplicity often expressed nostalgically in an age of complexity. In the end, Barrès' proposals reflect a desire to develop the full capacity of each individual. He is not a moralist. He proposes to sensitize man, make him aware of new needs, then teach him how to develop appropriate responses. It recalls Bergson's theory of creative evolution — or more dangerously — the underhanded manipulative credo of the modern advertiser. From *Un Homme libre* to André Maltère, Barrès' thought follows a logical curve. Freedom through self-enrichment; self-enrichment through sensitization, for the individual, then for the masses; this is the creed of Barrès who sees himself, not as a failed politician, but primarily as an educator.

CHAPTER 4

In Quest of 'National Energy'

IN 1897, Barrès published the first novel of the trilogy which bears the general title *Le Roman de l'énergie nationale.* The last two words of the title are evidence of an enormous step forward in his thought. The cult of energy had always absorbed him but his main concern had been with the development of this energy in the individual. Even in the case of André Maltère, he had seen the development of national energy as a consequence of the expansion of the individual. Now Barrès attempts to reverse the equation and show that strengthening one's sense of belonging to a nation is a vital prerequisite to the expansion of the *self.* He felt that his new opinions represented, not a contradiction of his old beliefs, but the growth and maturation of an intelligent man as he reaches his prime.

I   Les Déracinés

Massis claims that Barrès realized he had almost exhausted the vein of subtle analysis and that he sought to imitate Zola[1] by sketching out a broad social fresco. Barrès follows the fortunes and the misfortunes of a group of students as they learn the ways of society during the first years of their studies in Paris. They have differing ambitions but their actions are to a large extent dictated by the attitudes they absorb during the final years at the *lycée.* Barrès was later to claim[2] that his teachers had not awakened anything particularly important in his mind, and that he could recall from his school years only a feeling of boredom. This is not at all the situation described in the *lycée* of *Les Déracinés* in which Bouteiller is a powerful force whose slightest actions have an incalculable effect upon those under him.[3] Bouteiller unintentionally encourages the contempt of his pupils for the authority of the institutions under which they live. As a result, they grow up believing that honor consists in breaking the rules which are supposed to guide their conduct. Instead of acting for the common good, they think only of their own immediate advantage. Their individuality is not the disinterested egoism which seeks to understand and develop itself, but pure selfishness, unredeemed by freedom from outside pressure of opinion. The students seek personal success, but on other people's terms and so, to use one of Barrès' favorite expressions, fall too readily under the sway of the barbarians.

Although in his classes Bouteiller devotes himself to promoting the noble ideals of honor, responsibility, patriotism, solidarity and dignity, these ideals cannot prevail against his demeanor which stimulates self-assertiveness in his pupils. There can be no doubt though, that Bouteiller, like the majority of his colleagues, is sincere in his beliefs. Barrès never attempts to present him as an unprincipled Machiavelli, but rather as a scrupulous man who is corrupted quite unwittingly. Bouteiller stresses and practices, respect for the laws and acquiescence to social discipline. His major shortcoming is that his life is directed by abstract, rational principles. He persists in speaking of humanity in general terms, rather than envisaging society as a juxtaposition of widely varying individuals. As a result he fails to perceive that judgment of another's action must take into account the infinitely variable circumstances surrounding it, as well as abstract principles of justice. In an amusing aside, Barrès warns that Bouteiller is on the road towards fanatical intolerance; for after conceiving of a universal law applicable to all men, Bouteiller is very tempted to subject them to it for their own good.

Ironically enough, Bouteiller has much the same aims as Barrès. He intends to show his students the advantages of maintaining the social order, through the exercise of self-discipline. It is not his aims that are at fault, but his methods. He devotes his classes to stressing the inadequacies of philosophical theories, inducing in the minds of his listeners not only an overwhelming skepticism, but also an anguished nihilism which it is far from his intention to promote. When he finally re-asserts the notion of universal duty as preached by Kant, his students remain behind on the plane of relativism and uncertainty. Barrès has described the same crisis at some greater length in the *Culte du moi* trilogy. Here he confines himself to explaining that as the young students recognize nothing certain beyond the existence of their own selves, they affirm only their own right to succeed. In a lucid phrase, which he uses more than once, Barrès affirms that the major task of his generation is to pass from certitude to negation — without the loss of all moral values. Bouteiller's example, affirming as it does competitive individualism, does little to underpin the universal values already poorly affirmed by the outdated philosophy of Kant.[4]

After criticizing Bouteiller's ineptitude, Barrès briefly outlines the sort of educational method Bouteiller should have adopted. Barrès starts from the premise that Bouteiller's efforts to create a French citizen devoted to his civic duties are best effected by affirming regional tendencies. According to Barrès, local traditions are also French traditions. Devotion to one's home is also devotion to one's country. As the situation stands the students' local upbringing is contradicted by Bouteiller's teaching. Ambitious but naive, they are cast into the maelstrom of Parisian society.

Of those in the group Saint-Phlin remains the least influenced by Bouteiller, probably because he had spent most of his formative years with his family and had arrived at the *lycée* later than the others. With its roots deep in Lorraine's history, Saint-Phlin's family represents a principle of enlightened feudalism. After the manner of Montesquieu, Barrès stresses the best of the attitudes of the old feudal lords — their pride, courage, sense of duty, and responsibility towards their subjects. In Paris, Saint-Phlin becomes more aware of his traditional role. Despite the fact that he is studying for a "licence ès lettres," he prefers to study legal and social history, attempting to apply Taine's method to discover the origins of institutions and to predict which way they will develop. He adapts to modern circumstances in his association with those aristocrats who attempt to use their hereditary advantages of wealth and social standing to improve the lot of the working classes. Finally, after a disappointing love affair which reveals to him the emptiness of his life in Paris, Saint-Phlin returns to find consolation in his native Lorraine countryside. From there he follows the fortunes of his friends but does not intervene. They hear from him only when Racadot is guillotined.

Racadot and his companion in poverty, Mouchefrin, fail to win the position they seek. Of the two, Mouchefrin is the weaker. He attaches himself to the more energetic Racadot, sharing the latter's

hopes and his eventual decline. They are among the many who are
deceived by the "communism" — that is, the egalitarian spirit of
the *lycée*. As long as success depends solely on intellectual ability
they can equal their comrades; but in Paris, where so much depends
on upbringing and on social connections as well as on money, they
have no means of competing. To maintain his newspaper, his only
link with future success, Racadot exhausts expedient after expedient, each one more tenuous and improbable than the last. A
young Oriental widow, Astiné Arévian, the former mistress of
François Sturel, enables him to earn some money by attacking the
policy of the government in the colonies; but by being too greedy,
he loses even this grant. An attempt to borrow money off his father
fails; an attempt to steal some of Astiné's jewels fails. Finally, in
desperation, Racadot and Mouchefrin lure her to the Bois de Bou-
logne under the pretext of taking her to visit some of the ill-famed
haunts of Paris and kill her for the jewels she always wears.

Barrès does not adopt a totally unequivocal attitude towards the
murder. He is inclined to agree with Sturel that Astiné's lifestyle in-
creases the risk of such an occurrence, and that her violent end har-
monizes with her Oriental background composed of sensuality and
the sense of death. On the other hand, Barrès' social ideas tend to
make him approve of the argument that Roemerspacher, as a
responsible member of society, brings forward, that all lawbreakers
should be subjected to the full extent of punishment meted out by
the collectivity. Roemerspacher is forced to silence — partly by the
thought that not only has Racadot failed society — but society has
also failed him, and partly by a promise to Sturel not to pursue the
matter. There could even be some suspicion that Barrès is a little
more sympathetic towards Racadot than circumstances would war-
rant. When he claims that Racadot is possibly a more worthy representative of society than his companions, the first reason — that
Racadot's needs tend to maintain him on the plane of reality — is
quite justified; but the second — that he has shown awareness of
his social responsibilities by setting up a newspaper to serve the
needs of the group — is not quite the way Barrès had earlier
depicted the events. Racadot had set up the newspaper primarily to
serve his own ends; and the fact that it had profited his friends,
rather than him, was not his fault.

Barrès' general disapproval of the renegades whose actions damage society does not necessarily indicate approval for those who

accept the existing order and adapt to it. Renaudin, the struggling journalist who had preceded the rest of the group in Paris, plays a large part in the collapse of Racadot's dreams of success. Motivated solely by egoism, Renaudin is prepared to countenance any betrayal to increase his somewhat meager salary. In describing Renaudin's formation, Barrès digresses to criticize the more powerful figures of French journalism. His major complaint is that they are outsiders who do not understand the true interests of France. These people destroy themselves and others because they are not in harmony with the country in which they live and evolve. By their example they impress upon Renaudin that the most important goal is to make money whatever the consequences to others. Renaudin ruins Racadot in order to increase his income by 300 francs per month. Renaudin is also the first to recognize that the cohesion of the group he helps to create is not strong enough to reconcile the differing individualities of its members and abandons them to jump aboard Bouteiller's wagon.

It takes Suret-Lefort a little longer to discover his path; but in the end he proves to be more able than Renaudin. The latter has to advance by serving others, but this makes him enemies. Suret-Lefort does not serve others — he only uses them. He is quite unscrupulous and quite unencumbered by any kind of convictions. He can switch political beliefs whenever it suits him to do so; he regards religion merely as a useful method of keeping the masses in check; he considers the study of the law and of social institutions not a means of improving the lot of the people, but rather a means of making his mark in politics. Although he aspires to become one of the leaders of democracy, he fails even to notice the plight of the young girls who frequent the promiscuous atmosphere of the taverns until their untimely death. The most remarkable aspect of Suret-Lefort's development is that he rapidly develops a love of intrigue for its own sake. He does not really lead men, after the manner of Sturel's energetic ideal, but plays them off, one against the other.

Roemerspacher and Sturel are the main figures of the group, concerned with evolving a philosophy of life and action, but not with material gain. They represent in addition the most important aspects of Barrès' own development. When he reached maturity, Barrès often deplored the "poetic" temperament which alienated youths from the realities of life. François Sturel possesses these

poetic qualities to a remarkable degree. On the other hand,
Roemerspacher is a youthful version of the man Barrès becomes in
maturity. Roemerspacher's discussions with Sturel reflect Barrès'
own efforts to present a justification for the development of his
own thought.

Roemerspacher is characterized above all by his solid common
sense. He lives by Barrès' developed principle that a person is what
his surroundings make him. He seeks to achieve understanding by
impregnating himself with the spirit of a place, the better to com-
prehend its inner meaning. In contrast to Roemerspacher, Sturel
seeks to understand not his surroundings, but himself. Paradoxically, Roemerspacher will achieve understanding of himself
through the study of his origins while Sturel will fail to reach any
unity of character. The strongest "influence" in Roemerspacher's
thought is his meeting with Taine. For the purposes of the novel,
Barrès uses an actual meeting between Taine and Charles Maurras.
Roemerspacher begins by posing the problem that he thinks has
been created by Taine's generation. All faith and certainty have
been destroyed by the notion of relativity. The scientific method,
while an admirable tool, contains no ethical lesson within itself. In
answer, Taine does not attempt to solve the problem. Instead, he
goes beyond it, and imposes a moral ideal based on his own example. "I hope to carry on working right up to the end,"[5] he says even
though diabetes is visibly undermining his health. These words
cause Roemerspacher to take something like a leap of faith. He sees
that it is necessary to feel respect for the human dignity of others,
and for himself. The existence of individual differences becomes a
valuable commodity when every person is encouraged to develop
his own nature to its full extent according to an inner, instinctive
logic — the way a tree grows. Above all, however, Taine teaches the
acceptance of the conditions in which this growth must take place
— an acceptance which is not taught in the school system which
deals in abstractions.

After this interview, Roemerspacher chooses to discuss his
impressions, not with Saint-Phlin, who would have agreed with all
that has been said, but with Sturel, whose attitudes have already
developed in quite a different direction. Sturel has lost his chance
to let his true, inner nature unfold when he had failed to maintain
his relationship with Thérèse Alison on a secure footing. At a time
when he was open to any number of outside influences, Thérèse

might have consolidated the influence of Lorraine. Unfortunately, neither of them reveal their true feelings until too late. They illustrate Rousseau's comment about social intercourse taking place between two masks rather than between two real people. Sturel is vaguely conscious of the failure to communicate, for the letter he tears out of *La Nouvelle Héloïse*[6] to present to Thérèse refers to this very point. Mistrust and urbane politeness mark their stilted relationship. Thérèse's opinion of Sturel is confirmed by his adventure with Astiné, whose influence Barrès regards as little less than disastrous. Sturel's relationship with Astiné and Thérèse has been compared to that of André Maltère with Claire and Marina,[7] but there are major differences. André's relationship is fruitful, but Astiné poisons Sturel's life because he cannot assimilate her strangeness. What Bouteiller has begun Astiné completes. After his affair with her, Sturel is incapable of bringing his projects to a successful conclusion. Overwhelmed by the poetry of melancholy, secretly encouraged by the beauty of failure to reject success, Sturel turns into a rather febrile character. Unlike Roemerspacher, he is unable to wait patiently and let his inner self mature. Rather, like Philippe of the *Culte du moi* he needs to seek the pressure of some outside force, which often leads to contrary consequences.

When Sturel and his friend discuss what Taine has said, their attitudes reflect their divergent developments. Sturel is incapable of understanding what Barrès intends Taine to mean, namely that the value of the individual derives mainly from the social group of which he is a member, and that the greatest nobility is to submit oneself to the laws of the group to ensure its continuation. Sturel takes the opposite view, that the individual should be capable of imposing his own ideas on the group so as to make it develop into something new which will reflect the developments of his own personality. Sturel repeats in the main the ideas of André Maltère, while Roemerspacher is the spokesman for a development which is relatively new in Barrès' work, but which by 1897 forms an essential part of his intellectual credo.

It is Bouteiller who has the last word when, flushed with the victory of his election, he congratulates Suret-Lefort on having thrown over all trace of his local origins. Although he is the villain of the piece, Bouteiller's motives are not ignoble. He naturally rejects Sturel's excessive individualism and authoritarianism, but he is also incapable of understanding Roemerspacher's notions of the individual's obligations to the state. Both men have a sense of duty, but for Bouteiller duty consists in submitting himself to the established system and doing everything to further its existence, while for Roemerspacher, it consists in expressing himself and making understood his position within the state in the hope that in doing so he will sum up and clarify the ideas towards which the nation as a whole is moving. Bouteiller cannot accept this notion of development and change. He believes that the existing Republic is the only system that can benefit France as a whole and refuses to countenance any other. In the interests of the Republic, he lends himself to some shady political maneuvering; and although his star is rising as Barrès brings *Les Déracinés* to a close, his past will catch up with him in the subsequent novels.

II   L'Appel au Soldat

As befits a somewhat sensuous, sensitive individual, Sturel has left France for the delights of Venice, while the more practical Roemerspacher studies hard in Germany. Sturel is almost overcome. Despite its aesthetic appeal, the history of Italy is quite different from that of France and provides no point of contact to which Sturel can attach himself and use as a basis for action. He runs the risk of turning his energies inwards and destroying himself — of becoming totally rootless, seeking to fulfill himself in travel and foreign adventure instead of at home. A chance meeting with Thérèse, now Mme de Nelles, reminds him of France.

From the start, Roemerspacher uses the lessons of Germany to develop a purely French outlook. A German, he claims, believes that he must let himself be modified and formed by the world as it is. To the typically French idea that free will is the essence of man and that by it he is capable of renewing society, the German opposes the law of universal determinism. The Germans are blamed for being Naturalists by Roemerspacher, who evolves closer to Bergson. Submission to events leads the Germans to belief in a sort of Social Darwinism through which their barbarity is justified because they have proved themselves to be strongest through survival. This notion of the survival of the fittest which had led the character Racadot to try and justify his own crime, has already been denounced by Barrès, who believes in the value of all life and seeks to maintain an awareness of it by all means. In the end, Germany teaches Roemerspacher the same thing that Italy has taught Sturel. Roemerspacher becomes more aware of his native French qualities and he will use the method he has acquired in Germany to develop them. He will maintain a balance between the blind obedience to the past of the Germans, as well as the cavalier attitude towards the past of the authoritarian Sturel.

Both men have reached a definition of French nationalism which consists of "rejecting" elements of thought imported from abroad which tend to weaken the French character. At this point Sturel is called back to France by the publicity attached to the actions of Boulanger. Barrès seems to have been too embarrassed to admit that this typical Frenchman and heroic defender of French nationalism was half Welsh. After an outstanding military career, Boulanger began building up connections among leftwing politicians; and it was due to Clemenceau — with Constans' support (both of whom were later to bring about his downfall) — that Boulanger was appointed minister of war in 1886. Boulanger immediately distinguished himself by rousing republican declarations with skillful expression of socialist sentiments[8] and some timely sabre rattling, all of which inflamed the enthusiasm of the people. It was clear that Boulanger became a man to be reckoned with, but just what sort of threat did he represent?

Writing his account when he was embittered not only by the failure of Boulangism but also by the outcome of the Panama and Dreyfus affairs, Barrès was by this time steeped in frustrated antiparliamentarianism. It seemed logical for him to assert that the parliamentarians, all egoistically jockeying for their own advantage, should be afraid of the one man whose eventual victory in Alsace-Lorraine would put him at the head of a national movement which would sweep them all out of office. Boulanger, according to Barrès, was one of a series of heroes deliberately suppressed by men who preferred a dishonorable peace to the return of the captured provinces and their own oblivion.

Such charges were not new to the Boulangists, but had been made as early as 1885.[9] In reality, the politicians were not unaware of the plight of Alsace-Lorraine, but neither were they unaware of France's own unpreparedness and general unwillingness for war. The impetuous Boulanger in the War Office constituted an international danger which was removed when the government fell and he was packed off to command the 13th Army Corps at Clermont Fer-

rand. Large crowds turned out to see him go, perhaps also to prevent his departure. Barrès successfully captures the emotion and
excitement but he also catches some of the ridicule of the anti-
climax when a hot, thirsty Boulanger slipped out of his own car-
riage and escaped the attentions of the mob by riding on the platform of a spare locomotive. This man's subsequent career would
follow the same curve — enthusiastic triumph turning into farce.

In depicting this night of the general's departure, Barrès uses several of his fictional characters to assess the impact of Boulanger's
name. For Bouteiller, now a prominent ministerial figure
Boulanger is simply an empty puppet who does not know how to
use the power focussing on him. For Suret-Lefort and Renaudin, he
is a means of gaining power and fame. For Roemerspacher,
Boulanger is a symptom of a strong national aspiration for unity.
Sturel prefers to think of Boulanger as a person, while not forgetting the latter's symbolic value. At the same time he is uncomfort-
ably aware that if Boulanger attracts around him so many prominent people with such different beliefs, it is perhaps because he
lacks strong convictions himself.

Each adherent saw in Boulanger the means of attaining his own
desires. Naquet, the well known if not well loved father of the bill
authorizing divorce in France, believed with Barrès that the parliamentary system was unsuited to efficient government. A deputy
attempts to have an idea accepted. His proposal is ignored, not
through malice, but because it is swamped by government business.
The deputy then conspires to overthrow the government — to
become part of the one which takes its place — but he finds that in
the coalition of which he is part, not all the members accept his
views. Under attack from others seeking to overthrow him in his
turn, he waits until his position is solidly established so that his proposal will not cause his downfall. He waits too long and is toppled.
Deputies are not really elected to govern, says Naquet, but to do
favors for their electors. Barrès agrees. Both look to Boulanger to
sweep away a corrupt system. Rochefort, left wing aristocrat,
scourge of Napoleon, ex-communard, recently returned from exile
in Noumea had his own reasons for wanting to sweep away the parliamentary system which had condemned him. Déroulède, single-
minded proponent of all-out preparations to make war on Germany, founder to this effect of the League of Patriots thought that

Boulanger promised the possibility of destroying the parliamentary corruption holding back French efforts to attain a war footing.

These three were men of the left, even Déroulède, whose eventual totalitarianism should not be allowed to obscure his original republican leanings. As such, they appealed to Boulanger who never forgot the republicanism he had absorbed from his father, and whose task as war minister had been envisaged by Clemenceau as the republicanization of a rightist army. The bogus "Count" Dillon cut a stranger figure. He and Boulanger had first met at St-Cyr, and again in America where they had exchanged views on the American electoral and financial systems. Dillon became the financier of Boulanger's nascent party. He engineered Boulanger's contacts with the right, not out of any sense of conviction, but because that was where large sums of cash were available. It was through him that Boulanger, seemingly without understanding fully what he himself was doing, compromised himself with both the monarchists and bonapartists.

Boulanger's broad spectrum of support does lend credence to the view that he appealed through his personality rather than through his doctrine. It also explains why, when it came to implementing doctrines rather than attacking them, the party fell apart. Roemerspacher, momentarily abandoning his serious tone, lightheartedly approves Boulanger's acceptance of adherents of all shades of beliefs and is delighted to hear Sturel naively echo his sarcastic conclusion that national unity can result. Barrès implies that Sturel should have heeded Saint-Phlin. Unable to square what he knows of Boulanger with the ideas of a Lorraine countrysquire, Saint-Phlin returns home without pursuing the matters of the party any further.

Barrès makes it quite clear what he himself thinks of these events and of the personalities involved. He is highly suspicious of the shady Count Dillon, and deplores the count's efforts to curry the favor of the right. He detests Clemenceau because when Clemenceau withdrew the support of the radicals, he left Boulanger with little choice other than to seek a more rightist base of support. Barrès views Naquet with retroactive suspicion, deterred by Naquet's programs of social and economic reform and by his Jewish nationality. Elsewhere however, he expresses his continuing admiration for Naquet, a subtle, intelligent politician with the welfare of the people at heart.[10] Barrès' hero worship of Boulanger is tempered by the latter's obviously snobbish delight at being fêted in aristocratic circles. In Barrès' case, Boulanger's prime asset was his capacity to provide a rallying point in a divided country. His political program amounted to nothing more than a seizure of power, but this did not involve a usurpation of power by illegal means. Barrès was well aware of the executive advantages of dictatorship, but the establishment of the dictatorship was to be based on popular acclaim — on a virtual plebiscite — power should be attained by legal means, not by a *coup d'état*. Barrès' apparent regret in *L'Appel au Soldat* that Boulanger had failed to seize power is at odds with the sentiments he expressed at the time. He was convinced with Boulanger, that within six months the voters would give Boulanger by legal means what others were urging him to take by force. Barrès was proud to affirm that the general's revolution would be legal and bloodless.[11] It is only in his book that Barrès deplores the general's inadequate education which made Boulanger give too much weight to the anti-imperialist invective of a Victor Hugo and extol a vague humanism instead of a few well chosen nationalist ideas.

Boulanger also fails to find favor in the eyes of Saint-Phlin who, anxious to turn himself into a man of the soil, is suspicious of Boulanger's wide popular appeal and prefers that his local Boulangist representative show a keen awareness of local problems and quarrels. Saint-Phlin denies the essence of Boulangism because it is always the general's name that wins votes no matter what the constituency for which he stands. When Déroulède had stood in Boulanger's place in the Charente constituency, he had been at the bottom of the poll despite Boulanger's endorsement "A vote for Déroulède is a vote for me."

Roemerspacher, with his finely developed historical sense already regards Boulanger with little more than amused tolerance. Through Roemerspacher, Barrès is able to project a certain political acumen by predicting that the government will defeat Boulangism by revising the system of multiple candidacies and allowing a deputy to stand for one constituency only. Roemerspacher's attitude is curiously detached. While he does not recommend the *coup d'état,* he makes it obvious that Boulangism cannot succeed without it. Since Boulanger did not destroy his opponents first, he left them with sufficient strength to destroy him. Failing action on the part of Boulanger himself, his supporters should have acted in his name.

As for Sturel, his views seem to be dominated not by clair-voyance, but by the need to believe that the cause to which he is dedicating himself is inalienably correct. When there is a possibility of a *coup d'état,* Sturel praises the use of force. When the general makes it clear that he will employ only legal means for success, Sturel praises his restraint. Occasionally, Barrès is bitter and blames Boulanger for not being other than what he is. At other times he realizes that he himself is being illogical, and that Boulanger, if he had had the strength of character to take firm action at the decisive moment, would not have had that very empti-ness which made him all things to all men and attracted so much varied support. The main point Barrès intends to put across is that a moment came when the general forgot that he himself was the representative of French nationalism and of the best qualities in the French people. Instead of acting in the national interest, however, Boulanger acted selfishly. He was too concerned with his own plea-sure in the arms of Mme de Bonnemains and also too concerned with the judgment of posterity on his actions.

It seems to have been Barrès misfortune to be dazzled by figures who would subsequently disappoint him. He is now to contrast two of them — Boulanger and Bouteiller. The latter character becomes a political animal and loses in the process, that detached imper-sonality which wins over his pupils in Nancy. Barrès always persists in underlining a certain nobility in Bouteiller. Curiously enough, this nobility links him unwittingly, to Boulanger. Although they both gain fame in very different fields, both show courage and rise rapidly in their chosen professions. Both enter politics as sincere republicans, anxious to impress the stamp of republican virtue on their office. Both encounter cynicism and venality in others. Then their careers diverge. Under the influence of malcontents, Boulanger came to believe in the necessity of an enlightened despot-ism to purify French politics. Under the influence of parliamen-tarians, Bouteiller comes to believe that men should be governed by the Republic for their own good. Gradually, Bouteiller is caught up in a web of political intrigue. Barrès gives Bouteiller a dim aware-ness that a dictator can most easily take whatever action necessary. For Boulanger such a dictator would have had to be ensconced by popular plebiscite; but Bouteiller believes in a secret dictatorship of a few honest men behind a façade of democracy. Beyond Boulanger he sees the monarchist elements that Barrès himself opposed and he feels the need to combat Boulangism, while trying to purify republicanism. In the end, he falls into the same trap as Boulanger. It is a favorite idea of Barrès' that by attempting to defeat the enemy on his own ground, you become like him. The energy and enthusiasm of Boulangism were dissipated in electoral maneuverings. Bouteiller's energy and enthusiasm are stifled as he attempts to struggle to the top of his party and impose virtue from above. Barrès laments that two men, born to understand each other, should become through circumstance such irreconcilable enemies.

Boulanger's refusal of a coup, then his self-imposed flight into exile play into the hands of Bouteiller and his associates. The admiration of the people turns to bewilderment. Not everyone in the party agrees with Boulanger's decision and the rifts begin to show. As his fortunes become more uncertain, his sources of funds begin to dry up. Those who can begin to sever their connections. On the fictional level, Suret-Lefort, not out of principle but out of self interest, renews his relations with Bouteiller and concentrates all his efforts on the latter's re-election campaign in Lorraine without exactly renouncing Boulangism, but also without supporting it. Most of the remaining faithful are those who have no choice, like Renaudin, whose violent polemic has alienated everyone outside the Boulangist camp. Sturel, at a loss as to what to do, is pleased to receive an invitation from Saint-Phlin who, knowing his friend's weak points, suggests that it might be useful to Boulanger to be given a reliable firsthand account of the political situation in Lorraine.

The account of Sturel's excursion through the area occupies half of the second volume. The quantity of pages Barrès devotes to the topic gives proof of the important place it occupies in his mind. There is a slight displacement in chronology, however, for the events are supposed to take place in 1889 whereas it was not really until ten years later that Barrès starts serious inquiries into the fate of the occupied provinces. Despite feeble attempts to link the excursion to the rest of his novel, the whole mass appears out of place, only half-digested. At the time of Boulangism, Barrès has yet to be made aware of his own racial origins.

Sturel has been invited by Saint-Phlin because of the latter's desire to win a deputy over to his views on regionalism. Saint-Phlin is content to be patient, however, and for the first few days is quite happy to allow Sturel to use what he sees, to assess the future of Boulangism. His observations are not encouraging. The majority of people are strongly attached to their local customs and welfare. While ready to accept Boulangism as an accomplished fact, they cannot be counted upon to support a movement not in power, particularly a movement whose slogans are calculated to transcend local barriers. Barrès compares Boulanger's exile to the flight of Louis XVI who had been arrested by local peasants near the frontier. Despite a royalist tradition, the peasants had turned against the king because he had proved himself to be weak. For the same reason they will no longer support Boulanger. His only following then seems to be among the workers, a class which had uprooted itself from peasant tradition and was falling under the influence of Communistic ideas from which Barrès, as a parliamentary candidate, tried unsuccessfully to deter them.

Gradually, Saint-Phlin attempts to bring Sturel round to an appreciation of local phenomena. Saint-Phlin favors local autonomy, free from the interference of Berlin or Paris. He seeks to reinforce his local roots by studying patois. For him, Lorraine is a place in which to live permanently. For Sturel (as for Barrès) it is good to plunge himself briefly into the traditions of Lorraine to renew his energies; but he also needs the excitement of other traditions. Lorraine is a tonic rather than a way of life. Sturel and Saint-Phlin are closest to agreement only when they enter German territory where they both react against a heavy-handed authoritarianism. For Sturel, however, the Germans are destroying a French civilization, while for Saint-Phlin, they are destroying local initiative. The most Saint-Phlin will admit is that the region is closer in spirit to France than to Germany, or that the French aspects of civilization are superior to the German. For each of the friends the voyage is one of discovery, but each discovers a different truth. Saint-Phlin resolves to marry, settle down and devote himself to his estates. Sturel's conclusion is not so simple. For him, the lost provinces are a part of France which must be retaken at all costs for their own good. Boulangism offers the only means of achieving this. There is one other major difference. Saint-Phlin reiterates Barrès' old belief that the present is but a promise for the future, while Sturel tends to emphasize the present as a continuation of the past. Saint-Phlin is more constructive and open to change, while Sturel, though paradoxically advocating a *coup d'état,* is bound by conservatism.

When Sturel leaves Lorraine he unfortunately forgets all the conclusions to which his holiday has led him, and agrees to contest a
Paris seat despite his criticism of Parisian electoral districts for their
superficiality and lack of tradition. Although Sturel wins his seat,
the general results are disastrous for Boulangism. To try to prevent
the complete breakup of the party, the members make a journey to
Jersey, where Boulanger has retreated in the hope that its gentler
climate will arrest the increasingly tenacious consumption of his
adored mistress, Mme de Bonnemains.

Sturel is not particularly impressed by the meeting. The tech-
niques of parliamentarianism invade the party as orators speak, not
to shed light on the question at hand, but to satisfy their own vanity
and thirst for authority. Those who had been elected and were content to have their positions assured are distressed by the tendency of
the rest to seek power through extra-legal means. In the end,
nothing definite comes out of the intrigue. Even Drumont's candidacy is rejected because he is a racist, proof for Barrès that Boulanger has lost the thread of national instinct. Barrès describes
Sturel as rich, somewhat spoiled, and uninterested in economic
reform. On the other hand, Sturel shares Barrès' anti-Semitism,
also the hallmark of a number of fathers of Socialism. In rejecting
anti-Semitism, Boulanger also rejects a specific economic program
of which Sturel has tacitly approved when he deplores the exploita-
tion of the workers by the Jewish capitalist factory owner in Cus-
tines. The meeting ends with Déroulède insulting Boulanger, and
the five members of the executive committee handing in their resig-
nations. Boulanger remains alone, hoping forlornly that the French
people will recognize him.

Like Boulanger, Sturel is also alone, deserted by his friends
whose interests are different from his. Roemerspacher is interested
in his own career and in Mme de Nelles. Saint-Phlin, newly married, is still interested in his wife and in persuading Suret-Lefort to
propose in the Chamber some of his views on the necessity of
regionalist influence in education. Sturel's enthusiasm for Boulanger proves offensive to Mme de Saint-Phlin who cannot forgive his
open liaison with a divorced woman — and to Thérèse de Nelles —
who cannot forgive Sturel's contempt for Mme de Bonnemains.
Angry and awkward, Sturel makes it a point of honor not to aban-
don the cause. Seeing that he can do nothing in Parliament he
resigns his seat and devotes himself to promoting the Boulangist

weekly *The Voice of the People,* edited by an ex-communard, Pierre Denis. Meanwhile, other newspapers are publishing defamatory articles by disenchanted ex-Boulangists. Renaudin's article, followed by a duel, is an echo of the articles of Gabriel Terrail and the duels to which they gave rise.[12]

The novel ends with the general's suicide at the tomb of his dead mistress. Her death has left him weaker, not stronger. For Sturel, his campaign against the parliamentarians goes on. He is helped in the utmost secrecy, by Suret-Lefort, who has discovered that too many well established politicians stand between himself and success. Sturel has just begun his campaign when Boulanger dies. Boulanger has disregarded the appeal from his country. Sturel is to carry on the fight alone.

III   Leurs Figures

After the collapse of Boulangism, another affair arose which was to re-kindle, however briefly, right-wing hopes of sweeping away a corrupt parliamentary system. The Panama Company, founded by Ferdinand de Lesseps to repeat in Central America his triumph in Suez, had swiftly run into severe financial difficulties and was desperately dependent on favorable publicity and patronage. Despite enormous effort, the company had to go into liquidation in 1889. A number of shareholders, appalled by the staggering enormity of the loss should the project fall through completely, appealed to the government to provide the means to keep work in progress. Recalling an earlier report by one of its public works experts, the government showed little interest in saving the project, recommending instead that those responsible for the disaster should be identified and, if necessary, prosecuted.

This is how matters stand in the opening chapters of *Leurs Figures.* Boulanger is dead, and no other figure has proved sufficiently powerful to polarize the energies he had briefly tapped. His former supporters, embittered and vengeful, are yet incapable of undertaking constructive reforms. In a form of reaction, Sturel seeks scandal and destruction for their own sake, an attitude which almost drives him into the arms of the anarchists.

Suret-Lefort, on the other hand, is a happy renegade. Having successfully used Boulangism as a platform to ensure his election, he has suppressed his past, rallied to the men in power and is rapidly becoming an important part of the established power structure. He is one of the most flagrant examples of what Barrès calls a "parliamentarian." He has understood that a deputy participates in a sort of war game whose rules, though simple, are not immediately obvious. Firstly, a deputy is at all times fighting a re-election campaign, not only against candidates from other parties, but also against rivals within his own party. To outdistance the latter he must progress upwards in the power structure, and swift success here is achieved by understanding the second main rule: that votes are cast, not for or against ideas or principles, but for or against the minister in power. A master at covering himself against possible mistakes, Suret-Lefort develops the art of attacking the powerful without antagonizing them. In the process he loses all feeling for truth and honor.

Suret-Lefort and Bouteiller represent two different generations. The latter, while not overly scrupulous about the means he uses is utterly devoted to the republican cause — to the extent of compromising himself for it. Barrès recognizes that in his own way, Bouteiller possesses a certain nobility. He can never, for example, betray his party as Suret-Lefort betrays Boulangism. The irony and the pity is that as a result of the Panama scandal, the unprincipled Suret-Lefort is to squeeze his elder out of office.

Suret-Lefort is now the most conspicuous member of the small group which has sworn success before Napoleon's tomb many years before. He seeks to keep the main personalities together, not out of friendship, but because they may be useful to him. Although retired to the country and committed to the task of maintaining his estates, Saint-Phlin remains a powerful local influence who can help in Suret-Lefort's re-election. Roemerspacher, winning increasing respect as a talented academic can be a useful friend to count upon. Sturel, embittered by the political vacuum around him has turned into a vitriolic and intransigent journalist, and is acquiring more popularity and notoriety than ever before. Believing that he can control his friend in times of crisis, Suret-Lefort uses Sturel as a means of threatening or earning the gratitude of people in power. Of the four, only Sturel is ready to exploit the Panama scandal to its utmost. Suret-Lefort sees no point in upsetting a system he has learned to use to his advantage. Roemerspacher sees no point in destroying a system and creating a vacuum which nothing is ready to fill. He believes in supporting law and order because that is all there is. Like Roemerspacher, Saint-Phlin refuses to condone destruction for its own sake. He prefers to use Suret-Lefort to obtain small, practical reforms whose impact over the long term will, he hopes, prove out of all proportion to their apparent insignificance. Sturel, perhaps disappointed by the caution of his friends, perhaps gratified that the glory of the revelations will be his alone, undertakes the task of sifting out the truth of this murky affair.

Although there are some exaggerations, although some characters are painted blacker than they really are, Barrès' general thesis conforms closely to what is thought to be the truth of the actual matter. Many of his conclusions are based on conjecture but the circumstantial evidence is quite strong. When Charles de Lesseps appears before the examining magistrate, he affirms that while he and his associates have been able to construct Suez with their own funds, they have had to rely on favorable publicity as an incentive to the public to invest in the Panama project. Investments and good publicity have not come cheaply, and the company has been gouged by bankers, journalists and deputies. Barrès has already described in *Les Déracinés* how even Racadot has been able to squeeze a contribution out of Reinach for his struggling newspaper. More important, however, is the hint that deputies have been the willing victims of bribery and corruption. It is evident that at this stage, Charles de Lesseps is making the most gentle of threats — should the directors of the company be prosecuted, the government shall have some rather embarrassing situations to explain away. The agent of the company in these rather shady transactions is one Baron Jacques de Reinach. Through his background, Reinach fits in well with Barrès' picture of the transplanted foreigner, incapable of remaining true either to France's interests or cultural heritage.

The situation now degenerates into a series of more or less complicated maneuvers which usually take the form of a threat of accusation or revelation designed to protect the threat maker from the consequences of his own part in the affair. To scare his opponents, Reinach leaks a series of calculated disclosures to *La Libre Parole*. Not the least amusing episode in this affair is the spectacle of the violently anti-Semitic Edouard Drumont collaborating with one of the Jewish capitalists he despises. Barrès primly maintains that for the good of the cause, Drumont is willing to consent to almost any sacrifice. In return for the information, *La Libre Parole* excises Reinach's name from its articles; but no such agreement inhibits *La Cocarde* (although Barrès coyly refrains from disclosing the source of his newspaper's information). When Reinach commits suicide there are rumors that he has been poisoned, and even that his death is a fake; but in this case, the rumors can be discounted. Whatever else he may have been, Reinach was devoted to his family, and his death helps shield them from scandal. Reinach's son-in-law, Joseph, has time to burn any incriminating documents.

The troubles of those deputies who have been tempted and have succumbed are not yet over. An interpellation is slated by Jules Delahaye, an unscrupulous rabble-rouser hated by almost everybody. As he is pondering exactly what form his interpellation should take, emissaries of the Panama Board offer him just enough information to enable him to demand the establishment of a committee of inquiry — but not enough for him to be able to indict specific individuals. Barrès, claiming to base his judgment on a letter addressed to him by one of the members of this committee, affirms that there are three types of members — the careful ones, out to save themselves, or to save friends and above all the parliamentary system; the weak, who are afraid to incur the wrath of their colleagues; and the naive, who allow themselves to be duped by the others. The committee's attempt to gain judicial powers is blocked.

Struggles and insults continue. Five deputies, among them two recent ministers, have their immunity lifted. Clemenceau is denounced by Déroulède. Despite the furore there are signs that the more levelheaded realizing the danger not just to individuals, but to Parliament as a whole, are beginning to rally around the accused. Of the deputies, only one is convicted because he was foolish enough to throw himself on the mercy of the court and make a fatuous confession. The rest deny involvement, and the judges are in no mood to reject their protestations of innocence. The members of the Panama board are given the lightest of sentences, and even these are later revoked by the Cour de Cassation which orders their release.

Everything is returning to normal, and after he has finished describing the most exciting occurrences, Barrès returns to the fortunes and misfortunes of Sturel. Sturel is still sufficiently enthusiastic to believe that events create the man, that because the country is in need of a dictator to sweep away corruption, one will appear. Sturel's simple plan is to discredit the left, obtain a right-wing

majority at the following elections, and have the right wing resign
in favor of a dictatorship. Sturel is naive but Barrès is not. With the
advantage of hind-sight, he knows that even if the right wing has
triumphed over the left, which it actually has not, it is still too fragmented to undertake concerted action. In any event, Sturel does
not even have enough information to discredit the left. His frustrated anger drives him towards Fanfournot, the representative of
anarchism. Sturel makes a rather bitter comparison between the
anarchists and the "chequards" — the word coined to describe the
venal deputies. Both break the law but the latter have the knowledge and the connections which can keep them safe from the police.
There are other links between the anarchists and Sturel. Both wish
to overthrow the parliamentary system. Neither has any clear idea
of what to put in its place. Both realize that they have to rely on
their own efforts, that they will receive no help from the amorphous, apathetic mass of the bourgeoisie.

For a short whlie Sturel is tempted by the convulsive force and
direct action of anarchy and resolves on a series of newspaper articles, not so much to secure the conviction of the guilty deputies as
to stir up trouble and confusion in which, with the help of a bunch
of determined anarchists led by Fanfournot, he can organize a *coup
d'état*. As he is preparing his first article, Suret-Lefort comes to see
him, preparing the way for a visit by Bouteiller.

Panama has changed Bouteiller considerably. At the time of the
Boulanger affair, he had been strong and confident. Now he is tired
and anxious. He is fully aware that, noble though his motives may
have been at the time, he has compromised himself in Reinach's
affairs by accepting subsidies for his own election campaign, and a
well paid post in a Reinach-controlled newspaper. Despite
Bouteiller's decline, Barrès cannot help commenting on a certain
nobility in his decisions. His methods may not have been completely pure, but he has never deviated from his ideal, from his sincere belief that the public good is dependent upon the continued
strength of the republican elements in the parliamentary system. He
comes to Sturel, not to save his own skin, but because he recognizes
in Sturel and his friends strengths and qualities which can rejuve-
nate the republican party.

In his altruism Bouteiller contrasts favorably with Sturel whose
caesarism covers a selfish desire for strong sensations — and with
Suret-Lefort — whose opportunism and selfishness are plain for all

to see. Bouteiller rejects Sturel's suggestion that he put himself at the head of a *coup d'état* because he is committed to the republic (and perhaps also because he is intelligent enough to know that it will not work). The terms of his refusal, however, make plain a discrepancy between his teachings and his actions which has bothered Sturel for some years. As a schoolteacher Bouteiller had affirmed the existence of a universal moral which could not be bent to accommodate individual cases. In politics however, he refuses the role of a high-minded dictator who can purify the parliamentary system, on the grounds that the people are not ready for it. Because they have long ago perceived this discrepancy, Bouteiller's former pupils are mistrustful of him and cynical in their general dealings.

At this juncture Mme de Nelles, formerly Thérèse Alison and Sturel's former mistress, enters the room. She has made only brief appearances in *Leurs Figures* for the good reason that Sturel puts the excitement of politics well before the excitement of sex. Deserted by Sturel and disliking her husband she has turned to Roemerspacher and captivated him. Roemerspacher has also done her a great deal of good. He has imbued her with the solid qualities of Lorraine which had been masked by the brilliant cosmopolitanism of Paris and the nervous, ill-directed energies of Sturel. An unkind reader might find Thérèse cold and calculating. She does not hesitate to demand a divorce from her husband in exchange for persuading Sturel to suppress the articles in which he too is implicated. By a personal appeal she succeeds where Bouteiller has failed, because he maintained his arguments on a theoretical plane.

The people who gain are Roemerspacher, Suret-Lefort and Saint-Phlin. Roemerspacher will marry Thérèse, whom Barrès insists on describing as a charming, gentle young lady. Suret-Lefort becomes a power in the ruling political party. Saint-Phlin uses Suret-Lefort to put into operation his proposals for locally oriented education designed to give students a feeling for their own provinces, and which will later provide a solid base for French national sentiment. Saint-Phlin criticizes Bouteiller and Sturel equally. Both, he says, tend to think in abstract terms instead of restricting themselves to concrete proposals. In Bouteiller's case, he lays the blame on the foreign influence of Kant. In the case of Sturel he blames the ill-digested orientalism of Astiné Arévian.

The losers are Fanfournot and Bouteiller. Disgusted when Sturel backs out of the proposed *coup d'état,* and quite incapable of understanding his motives, Fanfournot takes the bomb he had intended to use to blow up the Chamber and tosses it haphazardly into a crowded restaurant. He is himself torn to pieces by an enraged mob. His death recalls the rash of anarchist atrocities after the Panama scandal, (the most notable being Vaillant's attempt to blow up the chamber for which he was executed). Bouteiller in his decline takes on a tragic grandeur which appeals to Barrès. He is deserted by the very party to which he has devoted all his efforts. Unlike other politicians who link ambition with utter lack of scruples, Bouteiller is incapable of turning against the party he has served. Rejected, despised, he is a touching figure in his solitude.

At first, Sturel too, seems to be a loser. He has sacrificed love for politics, then politics to the memory of his former love. As Bouteiller has been rejected by his party, Sturel has been rejected by his friends. He is not, however, so deprived as Bouteiller who has nothing to which he can cling, nothing for which he can hope except an unlikely return to grace in the eyes of the party leaders. Bouteiller's inner energies remain sterile because he cannot link them to anything. Sturel suddenly realizes that his own task is not to exploit outside energies — as in the Boulanger or Panama affairs — but to develop his personal resources as a representative of Lorraine and seek the harmony of his native traditions. Sturel is saved and will perhaps become a writer, as Roemerspacher had once suggested.

Roemerspacher and Saint-Phlin express some of Barrès' favorite ideas, but they arrive at them more directly than Barrès did himself. Sturel is more representative of the circuitous path Barrès took to reach his kernel of truth: regionalism and nationalism. Once this truth is attained it cannot be lost. Barrès can safely leave Sturel and go on to work out the implications of his new credo.

CHAPTER 5

Politics

W HEN Barrès linked his fortunes with those of Boulangism, his instructions to contest the parliamentary seat in Nancy ensured that he would have to grapple with large-scale social and economic problems. Socialism was not an essential part of Boulangism — the essence of Boulangism was the call for revision of the constitution — but Barrès had to link Socialism to Boulangism if he were to survive in his constituency. When the party fell apart, Barrès continued to uphold the nationalistic vigor that Boulanger had symbolized, and became almost by chance the first major figure to unite nationalism and Socialism. He continued his efforts to fuse the two from his election in 1889, until after his electoral failure at Nancy in 1898.

I De Hegel aux Cantines du Nord

Mixing popular philosophy and politics, this short essay is primarily an effort to promote a French brand of Socialism while discrediting other forms. Of the various types of Socialism Barrès is concerned with two, the collectivism of Marx and the anarchism of Bakunin. Collectivism contradicts Taine's method of refraining from imposing an outside ideal on people whose traditions do not fit them for it. It also contradicts Hegel's own method, which recognizes no fixed truth, insisting instead that everything is in a state of constant flux and development. After this succinct criticism of collectivism Barrès states that this is his "thesis" and proceeds to describe the "antithesis," anarchism which takes Hegel's method to extremes by threatening to destroy anything which does not develop quickly enough. Barrès finds it difficult to fault the theory of anarchism, confining himself to criticizing its lack of moderation and humility as well as its lack of organization.

Fortunately, the "synthesis" is at hand; and it has the added value of being purely French, not Germanic or Slavic. Proudhon is the descendant of Rousseau, Saint-Simon and Fourier and his ideas are in harmony with the traditions of the French people. They are also in harmony with Hegelianism for they represent, not a definitive solution, but a starting point whose results are unforseeable. The problem, as Barrès sees it, is to reconcile the values of authoritarianism and liberty, solidarity and individuality. The solution lies in the use of federation through contracts. A number of groups, each of which would be organized by a separate contract between its members, would join into the federation, thus maintaining their individuality while creating a strong nation. Barrès had before him the example of the Swiss confederation — as had Rousseau — although the latter had never succeeded in outlining the mechanism of the federation which was his eventual goal. Rousseau had given up his project because of the difficulties involved; but of course, Barrès does not need to worry about these. It is sufficient to pose a principle in harmony with French traditions and let time and evolution sort out the ramifications. The lack of conclusion which for some might be a weakness, is for Barrès the main strength.

II *The Nancy electoral program*

After his electoral defeat in 1893 Barrès continues to develop his ideas in the articles he writes for *La Cocarde*. When he stands for election in the Nancy constituency in 1898 he is able to present a coherent platform based on the articles he has written earlier. It is outlined in the appendix of *Scènes et doctrines du nationalisme*.

As a practical person, Barrès is aware that his program should aim, not just at enhancing the glory of France, but at meeting the people's most immediate, down-to-earth needs. Like all politicians at election time, Barrès is inclined to make his promises a little rosy, but as with the majority of his colleagues, his belief in the fundamental correctness of his basic propositions is sincere. His electioneering platform is the optimistic expression of his main beliefs, and an outline of some of the practical applications of his nationalistic tenets which, added together, total up to an increase in French prestige and glory.

Nationalism implies the exclusion of all foreign influences unless their power to harm is neutralized. Foreign workers, for example, are to be kept out. They send their money out of the country while taking jobs away from French workers and lower salaries and working conditions. On the other hand, if all foreign workers were to be expelled, there would be a surplus of jobs, and France's capacity to expand would be curtailed. Barrès' solution is to offer all jobs to Frenchmen first, leaving only the most unpalatable situations for foreigners. To offset the advantages of cheap foreign labor, Barrès proposes a special tax to be paid on every foreign worker. It is interesting that Barrès should adopt this solution, rather than insisting on equal pay for all workers, regardless of nationality. He often states that nationalism involves considering everything from the one-sided point of view of French advantage. He was concerned that French workers have sufficiently high salaries, but not with the welfare of foreign workers.

Barrès adopts a similar attitude towards foreigners in the higher echelons of society. He is thinking generally of the leaders of banking industry, many of whom had the misfortune of being Jewish — and are therefore guilty of not being French. There is some element of opportunism in the first stages of Barrès' anti-Semitism. It is most convenient to direct the anger of the people against these highly visible figures, and he always deplores the fact that Boulanger did not strengthen his platform by the judicious use of anti-Jewish feeling. Barrès calls for a transfer of their power into the hands of Frenchmen with the provision that the transfer should be a peaceful one, although he did not say how this was to be achieved. He is quite ready, however, to allow rich foreigners into the country to spend their money, much like permanent or semi-permanent tourists.

It is clear that Barrès' nationalism is steadily moving him in the direction of increasing state intervention, strengthening his links with Socialism. Protectionism is the first step. If French workers are going to be protected from the lowering of living standards induced by their foreign counterparts, then French industry should be protected from foreign competitors dumping cheaper products on the market. He does his best not to mention the fact that tariffs will lead to higher prices, although he does say that these will cause no hardship because the workers will have high salaries.

In all of his political appeals it is evident that although he is trying to net as many of the workers' votes as possible, his main target is the lower levels of the bourgeoisie. These not only comprise the largest segment of the voting population but are essential for his authoritarianism, depending as it does on their broad-based support.

In addition, his belief in this group as the inarticulate but sincere repository of the highest French values encourages his efforts to raise them to a heightened awareness of their role. Barrès the "realist" is aware, however, that education will not fill an empty stomach, hence his concern with the lower level bourgeoisie's material situation. From simple protectionism Barrès is led to develop a well-regulated Socialism which he defines as the physical and spiritual improvement of the poorest and most numerous classes. Some of his proposals have since been implemented and some are still under discussion. Insurance and retirement funds have now been set up for the benefit of workers. There have been some experiments in setting up worker's co-operatives — that is organizations to be owned by the workers who will not be paid a salary but who will split the profits among themselves. As applied to agriculture, this idea has led to the particularly fruitful development of the kibbutzim which Barrès foresaw as a Socialistic possibility.

It is not enough however, to ensure the welfare of the lower classes if other sectors of the economy remain under the control of foreigners or of uprooted entrepreneurs who have cast off purely French values. Barrès expresses the sort of anger that is expressed today against speculators who cause the market to swing wildly solely for their own gain; or against middlemen whose profits increase the cost to the consumer; or against the international cartels which control the resources of a country. Barrès does not state which specific modifications should be made, but he does invoke the principle of state intervention to correct these anomalies.

At this point Barrès realizes that it is time to counter arguments of the Socialists themselves, namely that they are an internationalist body which should resist being assimilated into any form of nationalism. They claim that the revolution from which their ideas stem is inspired by the affirmation of the rights of man in general, not of any particular man in any particular country. Barrès argues that there is a clear evolution from the international hegemony of the Roman Empire and the Christian Church, to the eventual breakup of empires into culturally homogeneous units betokening a specific nationality. Just as Barrès believes that true freedom involves accepting one's cultural origins, so too he believes that the

Socialists should accept the natural evolution of Socialism into nationalism, and with the infusion of Socialism, nationalism becomes not a return to the rigid forms of the past as Maurras advocates, but a dynamically evolving unit rooted in tradition and drawing strength from tradition to develop towards new forms. Having opened the door to the spirit of experimentation Barrès is quick to seize the advantages. Cultural hegemony leads not only to nationalism, but also to regionalism. The main purpose behind Barrès' regionalism is to free the provinces from the control of politicians in Paris who know nothing about the regions subject to their whims. When the provinces are controlled by people who have grown up there and who fully understand them, then they will prosper.

In addition to decentralizing and localizing government, Barrès takes other steps to turn it into a truly representative people's forum. He suggests that laws may be proposed by anyone, inside or outside government, and that regular referendums should be instituted. Naturally, there are gaps in Barrès' thumbnail sketch. His regionalism is not so solid as it looks, for any conflict of interest will be decided — probably in its own favor — by the central authority. The important thing is the spirit behind the proposals. Barrès believes in popular government because he feels it is the only way that cultural heritage can express itself in political and economic terms. Regionalism is one of Barrès' most original contributions to Socialism and is intended to enable it to avoid the danger of submitting all people to one uniform system. Federalism is to be a free, but inevitable choice made out of love for the federal state, France, to keep her strong.

III   *Scènes et doctrines du nationalisme*

All of Barrès' efforts foundered against the rock of the Dreyfus affair. Representatives of Socialism and those of nationalism lined up on opposite sides and Barrès was forced into making a choice. By this time his links with nationalism were stronger than his links with the Socialists whom he gave up as incurably internationalist. It might have been expected that Barrès would add a fourth novel to his series on national energy, based on the Dreyfus affair, which was certainly every bit as stimulating as the Boulanger and Panama crises. This time, however, Barrès preferred to gather together and republish the major articles he had written on the subject of nationalism.

Perhaps there was some disappointment and weariness in his attitude. The battle around Dreyfus had reached a stalemate unsatisfactory for both sides, and Barrès had resigned from his *Ligue de la Patrie Française* because instead of being a leavening, revitalizing the nation, the league had become just one more anti-ministerial faction caught up in the web of parliamentarianism. It is Barrès' avowed aim in all of the articles he has drawn together to rise above sterile political arguments and reach out, with his reader, to grasp the essence of nationalism. The notion should be one which transcends all political and social boundaries. The first short chapter is concerned with how Barrès himself has become aware of nationalism. It is his aim to show that nationalism can be the only logical goal of a person who is sincerely concerned with combining the quest for truth with a knowledge of himself. To this end he attempts to twist the major theoretical concerns of his time into a defense of nationalism. The notion of determinism had stimulated Zola into writing a whole series of novels apparently based on man's submission to his heredity and social environment. Barrès, however, looks beyond the immediate social environment to consider the whole cultural history of France. As a representative of French culture the individual has an important role to play, provided that he does not destroy his values by uprooting himself. Nationalism is the acceptance of one's determinism, claims Barrès in one of the arresting formulae for which he alone possessed the secret. Governed by his past, the Frenchman can act only as a representative of France. If he remains unaware of his past, however — or if he denies it — his actions are sterile.

Barrès hopes to form a nonpartisan organization into which he can attract people from all areas. Dreyfusard and anti-dreyfusard will submerge their differences in an expression of national brotherhood, as will freethinker and Catholic. Not particularly attracted by orthodox religion, Barrès prefers to project his capacity for belief on to his homeland. It is important, however, to understand his attitude towards reason and analysis. He accepts them as useful, though secondary tools. The choice of nationalism must be an intuitive one, grounded in love for one's country. Once the choice is made, reason and analysis may help in understanding one's background and strengthening it. Barrès makes his favorite comparison of a growing tree guided by its own inner necessity. He even goes so far as to claim that we are not masters of our own thoughts, that they are merely physiological reactions conditioned by our background. This notion must not be pushed to extremes. If considered as partially true it justifies Barrès' concern with regional education and with creating a nationalistic atmosphere in which the developing adolescent might be engulfed. As far as Barrès himself is concerned, despite lacking the advantage of a consciously regional upbringing his cult of the self has led him beyond the limits of the individual to an understanding of his historical antecedents. Beyond these limits individuality must lead to solidarity represented by the nation. The individual is ephemeral, but the nation, though it may slowly grow and develop, is eternal.

Such an all-embracing formula as nationalism thus may be applied to any topic. Nevertheless, the burning question of the day is the Dreyfus affair, so it is to this that Barrès turns his attention first. One curious effect of considering the affair from the elevated plateau of nationalism is that Dreyfus the man is forgotten. His humiliations and sufferings in a notorious French penal colony cease to have any meaning. Instead, Dreyfus the symbol is put on trial, becoming a center around which the divisive issues of the nation are focussed. Even for many of Dreyfus' supporters, Dreyfus is a useful symbol in their efforts to crush their opponents. Barrès recognizes that Dreyfus is a symptom of a deeper malaise and it is to this that he first turns his attention.

He is obliged to recognize that there are grounds for popular suspicion of the army but goes to its defense because he feels it will do no good for mistrust to persist between the army and the people. As long as the two factions are opposed, France's strength will be consumed in internal skirmishes instead of being used to form a barrier against German penetration. It is therefore imperative that the army be presented as a devoted body of men eager to weed the tarnished out from among them. Given these conditions, it really does not matter much whether Dreyfus is innocent or guilty. What matters is that the army thinks him to be guilty and takes the necessary steps to cleanse itself. Asked why Dreyfus should be assumed to be guilty Barrès replies that because he is a Jew he cannot have French national welfare at heart, but is a traitor from the line of Judas (forgetting that eleven other disciples had remained faithful). In arguments of this sort everything depends on the point of view. The facts of the case were far from being known at the time; and even today there is argument as to what extent Esterhazy acted alone, or to what extent he was a pawn covering for others. In the absence of definite facts to go on, being either for or against Dreyfus entailed an act of faith. As events turned out, publication of more facts tended to strengthen the dreyfusards and to weaken their opponents; there was perhaps a tinge of self-satisfaction in Barrès' claim that the full facts would never be known. In the interval, what factors will cause individuals to opt for one side or the other? Barrès' nationalist position is already known, so it is time to turn to his reconstruction of the motives of the "intellectual." For Barrès, the intellectual is an uprooted man who believes in eternal values and abstract ideals in the name of which he denies the right of legally constituted authority to rule over him. The intellectual is a cultivated man, a man without authority, yet who claims to bend authority to the conclusions to which his intelligence leads him. For Barrès, the intellectuals are acting in a vacuum, and not in accordance with fundamental national priorities. Their lack of understanding of their own origins threatens to sow chaos around them.

His attitude toward the religious outside Catholicism is revealing. Although he has no close attachment to the church he feels that Catholicism expresses what is finest in French nationalism. This is not to confuse nationalism with Catholicism, but merely to say that Catholicism leads naturally to an understanding of French nationalism. Barrès is suspicious of the monotheism of Protestantism and Judaism which he compares unfavorably to the panoply of saints which Catholicism has often adapted from the gods and goddesses of the pagan religions which preceded it. Clearly, for Barrès, Catholicism represents tradition while Protestantism represents a break from tradition in the name of abstract thought. An added cause for Barrès' suspicion is that the Protestants in Alsace-Lorraine tend to be won over easily by their Protestant counterparts in Germany. His conclusion, which he had already illustrated through the character Bouteiller, is that abstract, rootless thinkers fall almost invariably into graft and corruption when they make contact with the hard world of reality.

In a sense these comments serve as a preface to Barrès' coverage of Dreyfus' re-trial in 1899. He never claims to view the events with an open mind — only intellectuals do that. On the contrary, his mind is made up before he ever arrives in Rennes because of his

unquestioning confidence in the capability of those sitting in judgment, the army officers. If asked why he chooses the established
authority of the army over other forms of established authority,
Barrès would reply that the army officers have been formed in a
long tradition of discipline and self-sacrifice while the politicians
have freed themselves from tradition in order to pursue their own
selfish ends. Secure in certitude, it is easy for Barrès to claim that
Dreyfus oozes treason from every pore. The same absolute certainty bolsters Barrès' otherwise shaky efforts to prove that
Dreyfus must be a traitor because he is psychologically capable of
it. His affirmation that Dreyfus is doubly uprooted, from French
and from Jewish tradition is a plausible one, but it still does not
explain why Dreyfus should be so totally lacking in honor, unless
one accepts that only the French tradition can produce a sense of
honor. Even then there is Herzl's contrary argument that it was precisely because Dreyfus was a Jew attempting to gain recognition in
a different society, that he would have been incapable of transgres-
sing its rules.[1] Barrès seems incapable of understanding Dreyfus as
real human being. Whatever Dreyfus did he was guilty, either of
treason or of affording the opportunity to his defenders to tear
down the institutions he had sworn to uphold. For the same reason,
Picquart is as despicable as Dreyfus. He too has renounced the
established order for his own personal advantage. In the light of
this desertion Picquart's cultivation and intelligence are damning
qualities. Like all of Barrès' opponents he is consciously or unconsciously working against France in favor of her foreign enemies.

It is clear then, that Barrès does not go to Rennes to learn any
new facts. It is his hope that the trial will help stir up nationalistic
feeling, that perhaps something will happen which will lead to a
more felicitous *coup d'état* than Déroulède's hare-brained efforts.[2]
Nothing occurred.

Barrès was particularly attracted by the efforts of army officers
attempting to extend France's hegemony overseas. Such an officer
represents his ideal hero, the man of vision combined with the man
of action. He has to explain himself carefully, however, in view of
his other opinion that France will be far better off not to dissipate
her energies by taking far-off colonies, but to concentrate instead
on the reconquest of Alsace-Lorraine. He is even of the opinion
that Bismarck deliberately encourages French colonial escapades
the better to divert her attention. Why then, does Barrès allow him-

self to fall into the trap? It is not just a question of winning back Alsace-Lorraine, but of maintaining France's prestige in the face of other European powers. Barrès is infuriated by the loss of face over Fashoda, which he sees as yet another example of French weakness caused mainly by the opportunist politicians. He accuses them of sabotaging the efforts of the most competent soldiers to make France great, out of fear that a popular hero will seize power and tumble them into well deserved oblivion. For Barrès the politicians' failure to lend their support is too systematic not to be deliberate. They work to increase their popularity in France by whipping up chauvinistic feeling but withdraw on the brink of real action. As a result, French prestige abroad suffers and native peoples are encouraged to turn against their French colonizers, in order to be on the stronger side. According to Barrès, this sentiment has directly contributed to the death of Morès, an outstanding army officer assassinated in the course of seeking France's best interests, and undercut Marchand, already weakened by the failure of his reinforcements to arrive from Abyssinia and the shock of learning of the Dreyfus affair from Kitchener.

Morès and Marchand are frustrated but Barrès, third hero figure, Galliéni meets with greater success. When he is sent out to Madagascar, the island, third largest in the world and almost the size of Texas is in turmoil. Encouraged by the Protestant missionaries' affirmations of French weakness, the natives are beginning to develop into a dangerous threat. Galliéni soon takes care of this with a few judicious executions, then sets himself up as a benevolent despot, bringing all the benefits of paternalistic authoritarianism. What is noteworthy here is Barrès' wholehearted approval of brutal action which appears to clash with his belief in the benefits of French culture and civilization.

The discrepancy disappears when it is realized that in addition to being cultured one must also be a "realist." This involves having to make hard decisions when necessary. It is no doubt very regrettable that an example should have to be made of the ringleaders by executing them, but it is a necessary prelude to extending the benefits France has to offer. It also points up the advantages of having a dictator who must be in a position to make unpopular decisions necessitated by the general situation. Barrès is disillusioned by the failure to install any such figure in France. This was one reason for not turning the Dreyfus affair into a fictional sequel to *Leurs*

Figures. Other reasons are now apparent. While important, the
Dreyfus affair is just one aspect of the problem of nationalist
strength. The army, the colonies, the economy, the social problems
are just as important to the general pattern. In a novel dominated
by the Dreyfus affair Barrès cannot hope to handle all these diverse
elements. He compromises and reissues his most significant polemical articles dealing separately with each aspect of the situation.
Gradually, the reader makes the connecting links, grasps an overview of Barrès' program, and sees above all the need to back order
and authority.

IV   Les Amitiés françaises

This work tackles the problem of how to develop awareness of
nationalism in French youth. It seeks to amplify the minor proposals concerning local education that Saint-Phlin had persuaded
Suret-Lefort to adopt. In his prefatory remarks Barrès has some
interesting statements to make on education in general. He denies
that it is possible to teach a child anything in the sense that one cannot transform a child into something other than what he is. At best,
education can wake a child up and develop his potential a little
more quickly than would otherwise have been possible. It cannot,
however, modify a child's basic nature for this is a process that
takes centuries. In criticism obviously aimed at the republican ideal
of a universal education to fit a child to take his role in the family
of men, Barrès affirms that it is both impossible and crippling to
try to impose equality, by which he means uniformity, on people of
different backgrounds. Racadot in *Les Déracinés* has already illustrated the failure of such an attempt.

Taken at their best, Barrès' comments can lead to an enlightened
form of education aimed at teaching a child to accept himself for
what he is. There are too many insecure men of shallow intellect
who wrap themselves in the opinions of others because they have
no ideas of their own. At first sight, Barrès' notions on education,
emphasizing the stimulation of a child's imagination and creativity
appear designed to promote individual freedom. Barrès soon
makes it clear that such is not the case. Freedom for Barrès is the
freedom to conform. Individuality has to be taught how to fit harmoniously into its social context.

An important element in the essay is Barrès' realization that young children cannot be taught anything through the explanation of abstract logical principles. They are incapable of understanding a notion of universal rights or justice. Once this is accepted it can be turned to advantage by awakening a child's emotions and directing them towards a specific object. Reduced to the most simple terms, the two major emotions are love and hate. Barrès has no problems in choosing toward what he will direct the emotions. Love is for the French nation, considered not in the abstract, but as a matrix of famous people, events, traditions, places. Hate is for the Germans and their customs.

When Barrès applies these ideas to the education of his young son, Philippe, he readily succeeds in arousing the young boy's hate. The opposite element, love, is just as easy to arouse but perhaps more difficult to maintain. Satiety, boredom and misunderstanding can intervene and have an opposite effect to the one intended. Barrès first proceeds by trial and error to discover what excites Philippe. The son's education proves to follow much the same path as his father's. Philippe's enthusiasm is first aroused by the richness of Italy, as represented in Ariosto's *Orlando furioso*. Then, Barrès sets about transferring this enthusiasm to a French object and tells Philippe that the ruined castle of Sion-Vaudémont is just the same as the one Ariosto describes. On the actual site, Barrès takes the opportunity to explain how much the ruler of the castle had loved and helped France. He rather clumsily mentions that in return, the French had razed the castle and driven its lord into exile. Philippe is not to be allowed, however, to meditate upon the misdeeds of France and the advantages of independence for Alsace-Lorraine. He is rather tersely told that everything is for the best and that in any case Lorraine is now so French that it can not be changed.

Finally, Barrès is aware that religion is a powerful and effective force for binding people together in a homogeneous group. Only one sect is to be accredited, however, and even then, Barrès envisages Catholicism not so much as an international faith as one which reflects the typical French spirit. For the first time, Barrès devotes a substantial article to Joan of Arc, and we can see that he admires her, first because she incarnates the courage, simplicity and refinement of the French people; second, because she is of Lorraine; and third, because in a moment of crisis, she enables France by force of arms to affirm herself as a nation.

Events of the future were to prove that Barrès' education of his
son had paid off handsomely. When the invading German armies
swept into France in 1940 many right-wing French intellectuals
were in doubt. Should they welcome the Germans as right-wing
comrades who had made efficient use of their commonly held
totalitarian ideas and who could purge France and set her back on
the paths of greatness? Or should they reject the foreign invader
out of hand no matter what his ideas? Drieu la Rochelle collab-
orated for love of France (and was executed for it after the war).
For Philippe Barrès there was no doubt. Love of France was
equalled by hatred of Germany and he joined de Gaulle's free
forces in exile, under the banner of Lorraine.

Even with this success to his credit there are still some questions
to be raised concerning Barrès' view of France. He regards himself
as the repository of French tradition. In his writings, however, he
mentions Rabelais, Voltaire, Diderot and Stendhal only to criticize
them and deplore their influence. While he does not — until his
own claim to fame is secure — openly deny these figures their
Frenchness, there is no doubt of what his true feelings are. His
traditionalism then, is highly partial, and neglects important
sectors which many would consider to be typically French.

The reasons for these severe restrictions become clear when one
examines why he believes that education has to be based on emotive
appeal. In itself Barrès believes, life has no meaning. He sees the
world as chaotic and absurd, in much the same way as do the modern existentialists for whom full realization of the world's absurdity
is a stepping stone to liberty and dignity. For Barrès, however, the
notion of free choice and liberty is terrifying and there can be no
dignity in terror. Like Pascal, he seeks for a system to defend him
against the anguish of liberty, and he finds it in traditionalism.
There is a great deal of security in knowing that the old ways will
continue throughout one's life and after one's death. In a sense, by
forming one's children in the image of oneself one is able to defeat
death, at least partially. In his cult of traditionalism it is logical that
Barrès should prefer those who graft themselves onto an existing
tradition and reject the innovators who introduce instability into
human existence. Barrès accepts change; he realizes that he cannot
prevent it entirely; but he accepts it with reluctance, even when the
change is slow and gradual.

What becomes, then, of his doctrine of self-enrichment, the cult of the self? Barrès still affirms self-development provided that it is carried on with elements the same as those of which the self is already built up. The existentialists, or even Barrès' contemporary, Gide, regard the personality as a continuous reaction between successive elements creating something new. Barrès envisages the personality as being built up of homogeneous blocks, their total weight lending an imposing stability.

Given this attitude, Barrès has to take a hard look at his attraction to orientalism. Why should something so far outside his own tradition exercise such a pull on him? He realizes that orientalism represents excitement and passion, the necessary antidote for a person who has steeped too long in serenity. Happiness lies not in repose, but in a compromise between two extremes. Orientalism thus becomes a necessary stimulant as long as it is restricted to small doses. In large quantities it threatens to poison the system of the person who becomes addicted to it. One of Barrès' reasons for hating and fearing Germany is that he believes German culture to contain an admixture of exoticism too strong for the French soul if not filtered out. Novelty is not rejected out of hand. It is accepted but made to conform, or else discarded.

As Barrès' answer to the absurdity of life, *Les Amitiés françaises* entails, not a denial of his previous beliefs but a re-casting of them so that the more radical features are softened. The cult of the self continues but in accord with a known pattern. Socialism persists but it is to be determined by the past instead of itself determining the future. The Dreyfus affair certainly hastens Barrès' changeover to the right. When the representatives of Socialism and nationalism line up on opposite sides, Barrès is forced into making a choice. By this time his links with traditionalism are too strong to be denied. He moves right to defend France, and also his own peace of mind.

CHAPTER 6

Alsace-Lorraine

F ROM the very beginning of his career Barrès longs for the return of the lost provinces. Even in the *Taches d'encre* he is able to speak of reconquering them with "a little blood, and some greatness of soul."[1] As his career progresses his insistence on their return grows more shrill as the provinces develop an increasingly important role in his thought. In the article just quoted, Barrès can recognize the greatness of German thought and accept its influence on French life and letters. Xenophobia first creeps into his writing as a useful tool for uniting the disparate factions of Boulangism, but does not at first extend very far. He imagines that the recuperation of the provinces might be effected by "a policy of dignity and vigorous diplomacy."[2] He is warm in his expressions of desire for reconciliation between France and Germany although he cannot imagine it taking place until the problem of the return of the provinces has been solved.[3] Political failure embitters Barrès and causes him to take his xenophobia more seriously. In 1894 he defends French Socialism (as opposed to other brands) because of its moral superiority.[4] The continued occupation of the provinces now comes to symbolize for Barrès an unacceptable French weakness. France is weak because she makes no effort to resist; but the conquered provinces, reacting against German brutality, maintain their strength and vigor. Thus the provinces, if they are returned, will be a major force in regenerating France. Disappointed with parliamentarianism, Barrès turns to the two provinces as a source of French values, holding up under determined foreign attack. His aim is twofold — to help stiffen resistance in the conquered provinces and to stiffen French morale by describing their struggle.

94

I   Au Service de l'Allemagne

The novel opens with an attempt to determine the extent to which the inhabitants of Alsace-Lorraine have retained their regional characteristics. *Les Déracinés* has already shown how the artificial climate of Paris can spoil the healthy temperamental and cultural development of centuries. Will the imposition by the Germans of an equally artificial climate destroy the roots of culture in Alsace-Lorraine itself? The reassuring conclusion is that despite its vigorous action, German culture succeeds only in awakening an aggressive sense of awareness in the majority of the native population. German laws, despite a certain superficial appeal, cannot suborn the French mentality. The reason Barrès gives is that German laws are aimed at people in a lower state of development than the French. Germans stick strictly to the letter of the law and within these limits act basely and selfishly with no indulgence or regard for others as individuals. The French, on the other hand, possess to a high degree the notion of honor which transcends the letter of the law, the better to impose the spirit of generosity. Another more serious question, is the extent to which the French, through being forced to use devious means to uphold their national characteristics are actually destroying themselves by creating a climate of hypocrisy and confusion, as Boulangism had done when it had attempted to engage parliamentarianism on its own ground. Trained in the art of mental judo, using the enemy's subconscious attitudes against him, the local population might be flirting with an hypocrisy necessary in an occupied country, but one which might eventually lead to a dulling of that sense of honor which is the major French trait.

At the center of the work are the chapters devoted to Sainte-Odile and its significance. Steeped in history, the hill and its ruins form a particularly striking site from which to contemplate the countryside lying under German domination. For Barrès, who has not cut himself off from his roots, the hill of Sainte-Odile is a civilizing force which will eventually absorb all the waves of barbarian influence and retain, through an infinite number of changing forms, those elements on which its qualities of civilization depend. Barrès establishes various sets of synonyms. The terms "German," "Protestant" and "barbarian" go together as do the terms "Celtic," "Roman," "French," "Catholic" and "civilization." Finally, in a passage which recalls the resolution of Philippe in *Un*

Homme libre, Barrès explains how devotion to Sainte-Odile can inspire a discipline. Using vocabulary and ideas borrowed from Loyola, Barrès proposes creating a system of direction through a series of spiritual exercises and meditations suggested by the hill. In his call to set up a barrier to the influx of German Protestant ideas, Barrès recreates the tenor of the Counter-Reformation. He concedes that this is a somewhat complicated structure of ideas to emerge out of contemplation from a hilltop and agrees that there is perhaps an element of wishful thinking on his part. The chapter ends on a note of cautious optimism. The hill of Sainte-Odile is a promise for the future. Its existence throughout history guarantees that it will continue to exist and represent the forces of civilization it has always represented; but the hill gives no hint of how this will be achieved. Barrès remains quite ignorant of how his hopes will be fulfilled.

These are the main problems Barrès faces when he undertakes his study of Franco-German relations in Alsace-Lorraine in the closing years of the 1890s. In the summer of 1898 he had the good fortune to be introduced to Dr. Pierre Bucher, whose personality and ideas are to be found with only slight modification in Paul Ehrmann, the Alsatian doctor who is obliged, if he wishes to remain in Alsace, to perform his military service for Germany. When Barrès was undertaking some of the research for the novel there occurred a literary event which helped to crystallize in his mind the form which his major thesis should take. In 1901, René Bazin published *Les Oberlé,* a study of an Alsatian forced by economic necessity to come to terms with the German occupiers. Bazin maintains that if a young man wishes to keep his honor intact, there is only one solution — flight across the border. This is a conclusion which, after his conversations with Pierre Bucher, Barrès cannot condone. The major thrust of Barrès' novel is devoted to demonstrating that honor, if properly understood, leads an Alsatian to remain under the German yoke at whatever cost. The aim is twofold, firstly to persuade local inhabitants to remain in German held territories; secondly to persuade the French that these people should be respected and not considered as collaborators. The bare bones of his argument may be found in his article on *Les Oberlé*[5]; but his novel takes the idea and clothes it in living form. Barrès believes that logical explanations are not the proper way to convince people. They may prove that the man who proposes them possesses a sharp intelligence, but they will not necessarily be palatable. Barrès prefers to try and touch his readers' emotions and plant in their minds an impression which will grow and develop.

The vehicle Barrès chooses to convey his sentiments is Paul Ehrmann. Putting himself into his won novel, Barrès first meets Ehrmann at an inn during the course of a trip to question local lawyers concerning the effects of German laws on the local inhabitants. Unfortunately, Barrès is with Pierre Le Sourd. The latter is well named for he appears to be quite deaf to the arguments of other people. Ehrmann, who is about to start his six month period of military service with the German army is upset by Le Sourd's dismissal of him as a traitor and a coward. The scene is not quite so vivid as in one of the early, rough sketches in which Ehrmann seizes hold of a carafe, presumably to hurl it at his adversary; but the scene is better, toned down, particularly in view of the self-control that Ehrmann demonstrates in other situations. Vaguely amorous complications between Ehrmann and Mme d'Aoury, roughly sketched out in the *Cahiers,*[6] are likewise toned down in the final version of *Au Service de l'Allemagne,* and simply become expressions of admiration on Ehrmann's part for the vivacity and charm of a typical Parisienne. Le Sourd's insult can evidently be wiped out only through a duel which, much to Le Sourd's chagrin, Ehrmann wins easily. Despite his admiration, Barrès professes to be unsure of Ehrmann's deepest sentiments. There are times when the outlook he expresses is purely French; yet there is also a certain heaviness and seriousness about him which suggest the German temperament. As Barrès accompanies Ehrmann and his friend from the house to the railway station, he is sorry to have to repress the questions which rise to his lips and which there is no time to ask.

After this incident Ehrmann flits in and out of Barrès' life. He appears in a student brawl in a café, where Barrès witnesses him half strangle a huge German. On another occasion, Barrès sees him leaving the barracks, but Ehrmann gives no sign of recognition, obviously displeased at being seen in a German uniform. At last, after his long meditation on the Sainte-Odile summit, Barrès meets Ehrmann again, happy to be reintegrated with civilian life after his release from the army and more willing to tell his own story. It is a simple one without any particularly unusual or dramatic incidents. It becomes immediately clear, however, that Ehrmann suffers, not so much from army life as from being a Frenchman in the German army. This is part of the price he must pay for remaining in Alsace; and his reasons for remaining are strong. From a personal point of view he is chagrined by the thought of uprooting himself and leaving behind his heritage. In Alsace he feels at home, and through work and service he can give his life a meaning in harmony with his surroundings. In France he would simply be another refugee struggling against the indirect resentment that most refugees encounter. From a more altruistic point of view, he realizes that he is needed more in Alsace than in France. To emigrate is to allow the Germans to take over all the industry, commerce and services without a struggle. As long as there are French people in the occupied territories France will have an excuse for making war to win them back. Ehrmann stays on therefore, despite the prospect of unpleasant experiences because he feels it is his duty.

The story of his army service shows how, starting from his moral resolution, he gradually forges for himself a clear line of conduct. The first step is his decision that instead of simply resigning himself to military service he will attempt to win his companions' esteem by becoming a first-class soldier. The next step is to seize every occasion to impress them with the understanding that *because* he is French he is superior. This decision leads him to an analysis of various types of Germans. The Prussian for example, is a hopeless case. He is petty, jealous, narrow-minded, legalistic, impolite, uncultured, simplistic, dogmatic and semi-alcoholic! Representatives of other regions — as the Saxon or Bavarian — are viewed as more sympathetic, although they lack a full understanding of their own true natures. These are the ones whom Ehrmann hopes to raise to a more highly conscious level of cultivation by setting before them the example of his own acts. What are the specific aspects of French superiority? The French have wider culture, deeper sensitivity, an instinct for the right action and a regard for the welfare of others which makes them take into account extenuating circumstances and other nuances. When according to the Prussian rule of conduct, he can have denounced his comrades, Ehrmann helps them instead. He uses every occasion to point out to them the barbarity of their own system — their reliance on force instead of honor, their insistence in religion, on the puritanical work ethic and horror of sin, instead of on the notions of generosity, sacrifice and heroism.

Ehrmann is the answer to Barrès' question on Sainte-Odile as to by just what means the French spirit will overcome the German invaders. Ehrmann is the French spirit in action. He relies not on Catholicism or religious fervor (which are weakened), not on the military spirit which the Germans possess to a higher degree, not on an emphasis on economic advantages which will tend to favor unification with Germany — but on his own culture. Whether one chooses to leave Alsace or to stay either decision runs the risk of being unproductive. Cut off from one's roots one may wither, but one may also be destroyed by the inevitable contradictions a defeated nation must face. Ehrmann largely avoids sterile speculation and as a result his actions are creative, yet at the same time representative.

The final episode of the novel is prophetic. Ehrmann's commanding officer has come to look upon him with admiration, and even a sort of friendship. On the point of completing his service, Ehrmann deliberately destroys the edifice he has built up and is happy that they should both appear in what he considers their true roles as eternal hereditary enemies. The attempt to promote a civilizing influence is forgotten in favor of naked aggression. This episode reflects Barrès' belief that the French must negotiate from a position of strength. He explains in the postwar preface that it is honorable and desirable to civilize and absorb the Germans, only after the Germans have been smashed. At the last moment Barrès drops his mask and reveals that he equates the peaceful ideals of civilization with a shrill aggressive nationalism.

II   Colette Baudoche

Love between enemies is the theme of this novel. The Franco-Prussian war has been fought almost forty years earlier; the soldiers who had occupied the provinces have for the most part gone home and been replaced by administrators and schoolteachers. The war continues not against the French army, but against French culture. Barrès bases his novel on accounts of actual marriages between the invaders and young local girls.[7] Colette is nineteen years old and has lived all her life under the German occupation. Her major source of knowledge for French life and culture is her grandmother, Mme Baudoche, who had known Metz before the disastrous French surrender. Without being fully conscious of it, Mme Baudoche is a repository for that particular French way of life which the Germans attempt to stifle. Thanks to her constant influence Colette has grown up in the pure French tradition instead of becoming some sort of half-caste adrift between two cultures. Under the stifling atmosphere of heavy-handed German chauvinism Colette is more French than if her family had uprooted itself and settled in another part of France as virtual strangers.

It is interesting to compare her to Sturel, who had been separated from his local heritage, in part because he had never experienced the solicitous presence of an older person able to incarnate this indigenous culture. Sturel let himself be attracted by foreign influences in the person of Astiné Arévian. Faced with the same temptation, how will Colette react? Her unprepossessing suitor, Dr. Frédéric Asmus, to give him the title which is his due has come to Metz imbued with a sense of patriotic duty to teach young French children to be good Germans. He is boastful, humorless, tactless, overly concerned with titles, money and other outward displays of superiority; but all this is partially redeemed by an immense naivety and by a desire to be liked and do the right thing. He soon shows that he shares his countrymen's capacity for eating and drinking, and their incapacity for understanding the subtle malice with which the French comment on German behavior.

To some extent Asmus is an atypical German in that he feels an inferiority complex. He has accepted his fiancée's assertion that there is a void at the center of his life which needs to be filled by experience of some kind. He is in the same sort of position as was Sturel who goes to Paris without the solid buttress of a strong local culture. Like Sturel Asmus is wide open to foreign influences. In this case, however, Barrès approves of the influences because they are French.

Barrès introduces here what he considers to be one of the most important functions of Alsace and Lorraine: to act as combined filter and catalyst straining out German influences from across the Rhine and accommodating them to the French outlook. He goes further and claims that French culture has always exercised a powerful attraction on its barbarous neighbors. He believes that there can be only two attitudes on the part of Germans towards this attraction. They can be aware of it and reject it violently like the majority of Asmus' drinking companions, or like Asmus himself they can turn to French culture to remedy their sense of inadequacy. Asmus learns to relax and enjoy what Barrès calls the unaccustomed hygiene of the French way of life. In place of heavy German foods Mme Baudoche substitutes light French dishes, wine instead of beer, eggs instead of meat; and the change in diet seems to sharpen Asmus' sensitivity. Then she speaks to him at length of Metz and its history. Asmus thinks that he is practicing his French but in fact he is being confronted with a new culture and gradually becoming disposed to accept its superiority. As his education progresses he realizes that Colette's culture is a unified whole because she has absorbed it instinctively and has never had to learn it whereas his own attitudes are false, because they have been acquired by an intellectual effort and have no deep roots either in his own life or in the life of his nation. For the first time, Asmus learns how to create a deeply meaningful existence for himself through the association of strongly held sentiments with the objects of civilization around him.

One of the main turning points in the novel, when Asmus' development receives a fresh impetus is his trip across the border to visit the French town of Nancy. For the first time, in Nancy, he feels French civilization instead of trying to assess it intellectually, and Barrès suggests that at the root of Asmus' understanding there is a growing attachment for Colette. Asmus attempts to carry out undertakings which he knows will please her, all of them concerned with halting the repressive Germanization taking place and with favoring instead the continued development of French culture. As he proves his friendship the Baudoche family gradually unbends. They allow themselves to be seen with him in public and finally accept his invitation to one of the village fairs in the locality. Nature exerts its charm upon the two young people, and as they take leave of each other, Asmus attempts to give her a kiss.

From this point on Barrès is concerned with the question of whether Colette should marry Asmus. In point of fact there is really no question at all in Barrès' mind. He has already shown what he thinks of mixed marriages in his descriptions of Colette's neighbor, the unhappy Mme Krauss, embittered by her distasteful marriage to a German electrician. Tharaud recounts Barrès' hesitations over whether Colette should return Asmus' kiss before deciding against it, and also indicates how Mistral had reproached Barrès for giving Colette a somewhat incongruous attitude, pointing out that it would be natural for the young couple to work together to create a new future.[8]

Barrès makes Colette think not of the future, but of the past. His attitude recalls that of Colette's grandmother, who is incapable of sharing the pleasure of the two young people on a country excursion because she is burdened by her memories of the time when the French had been in control. Colette submits herself in spirit to the judgment of a group of old women who know only how to dwell on the past because they have no future. Her decision is reinforced by the ceremonies of the "Day of the Dead," when the fallen French soldiers are honored. Barrès' description of the ceremony in Metz cathedral is strangely echoed by Sartre's description of a similar festival in *Les Mouches.* The dead swarm out of their graves and surround the people, forcing them into their old preset roles which constrict their daily lives. Barrès does not, of course, notice the constriction. He speaks instead of the strength of a French tradition, Corneille's ideal of honor to which Colette sacrifices her personal interests. Barrès sees marriage as a form of submission on the part of the woman. Colette has already known the triumph of converting a representative of Germany to French civilization, now her duty must be to bear French sons who will win back the lost provinces. In the end therefore, she rejects Asmus' offer of marriage because the strongest elements of French tradition militate against it.

The notion that French civilization illumines the rest of Europe has been a cherished belief on the part of French writers ever since the eighteenth century. Barrès is particularly susceptible to this point of view because of his insistence on the value of strongly rooted French traditions. The proposed marriage between Colette and Asmus symbolizes the possibility of a union between their two countries. France could supply some sort of leavening to the heavy German temperament, while Germany could supply the strength and energy that the French unfortunately so often lack to uphold their ideas.

Some thirty years later, under the heel of yet another German occupation, Vercors is to develop the same ideas only to reject them in *Le Silence de la mer,* where the notion of love between two enemies is repulsed as despicable collaboration and the two countries viewed as irreconcilable enemies. For Barrès it is permissible for France to demonstrate her superiority by changing the German outlook, but it is to be clearly understood that she should be the dominant partner. He cannot accept compromise from a position of weakness. Instead, he is obliged to maintain a somewhat uncomfortable *status quo* through the harsh assertion of the unchanging values of French tradition.

CHAPTER 7

Exoticism

BARRÈS' attraction to the exotic spreads over his entire career and appears in his work in many forms, whether in the fictional character Astiné Arévian of *Les Déracinés,* or the real-life dancing dervishes of *Une enquête aux pays du Levant.* As his career develops, his attitude to exoticism changes. *Du Sang, de la volupté et de la mort* published in 1894 is, as Miéville points out, "a collection of widely differing studies whose dominant tendency is the exaltation of the ego through all sorts of more or less carefully prepared excesses."[1] When his thoughts change his attitude towards exoticism changes too. Caramaschi claims that the execution of Venice in *Amori et dolori sacrum* is the necessary result of Barrès' development of the cult of tradition.[2] The four works treated in this chapter represent Barrès' most sustained excursions into exoticism and provide an overview of the development of his ideas.

I   Du Sang, de la volupté et de la mort

Although in *Le Jardin de Bérénice* Barrès had just proclaimed his nascent awareness of the unconscious wisdom of the masses, the dedication of this collection of sketches *Du Sang, de la volupté et de la mort* to his dead friend, Jules Tellier shows that Barrès still shares the Romantic view of the ignorance and insensitivity of the masses. Barrès admits that he has opposed the posthumous publication of his friend's verses in the belief that a man of integrity keeps his views to himself without seeking recognition or fame from an uninspired public. The obvious question then arises, what makes Barrès himself embark upon a writing career? The answer is, a combination of the desire to formulate his thought clearly and the urge to project his will upon other people. Despite his complaints that the public remains intractable, Barrès seeks to impress his own ideas on the masses. In doing so he runs into the curious paradox which affects writers and politicians. They claim to be the inspirers of the people, yet when they gain a position of authority they have to make themselves the people's servants. Barrès prefers not to probe too deeply into this contradiction, but he shows by his attitude towards the death of Jules Tellier that he is aware that his friend has escaped the agony of conflicting interests. Barrès' loss lies in his being deprived of a friend and companion with whom he can discuss these matters. Tellier's death diminishes him because it takes away the opportunity to develop certain aspects of his own ego. The composition of these stories is, in a sense, an attempt to replace conversation with Jules Tellier.

The first section of the book explores what happens when people are wrenched out of the even tenor of their lives. Called from Dresden to Toledo by her half-brother, the "amateur d'âmes" of the story's title, Pia cannot withstand the confusion of forces which batter her psyche. Delrio's influence over her and his careless handling of it, is a restatement of Philippe's influence over Bérénice.[3] Another passionate woman of extremes, Violante,[4] breaks away from her mode of life the better to realize her own potential. As for her lover, he too is a typical Barresian young man. Sensitive and predisposed to melancholy, he is excited by the knowledge that what he loves best must disappear. He is like the king of Thulé of the title who destroys a treasured possession in order to enjoy a fleeting sensation. The story illustrates Barrès' curious dual attitude at this stage to notions of death and tradition. His reaction to death is originally one of horror. He plunges into destruction because he feels that he cannot in the end escape it.[5] It is true that Violante will live on in the memories of those with whom she has come into contact, but this sort of immortality is too tenuous really to satisfy Barrès. It is but a short step to his belief that the individual, too puny to exert an appreciable influence on the future by his unaided efforts, should work through an already established tradition.

At this stage, however, Barrès is not yet ready to take the step which will unite him with the unconscious traditions of the common man. Still under the influence of the Romantic ideal of the artist as superior being, Barrès repeats the assertion that one should hide one's opinions from the vulgar mob. He seeks privacy in order to cultivate as many different forms of his ego as possible. He will later denounce the chaos to which this uncontrolled cultivation leads and praise the tight control that traditionalism exercises over the way in which the ego may be allowed to develop. Barrès cannot defeat death by himself, but he can defeat it through tradition.

So far, Barrès has described the effects of love in its various forms. Now he turns to the opposite emotion, hate, groping towards an important social concept. All through his political life Barrès desired to be recognized as a mass-leader and sought to manipulate the people through their baser instincts, calling himself a realist as he did so. Manifestations of hate for him are important sociological signposts for the use of the would-be leader.

From the first section which deals with characters who in some way or other develop a theory of passion Barrès passes on to Spain, a country which exudes passion from every pore of its being. As if to underline the importance of the contrast between the life of passion and the melancholy which has been prevalent in his first novels, Barrès chooses to imagine how he might have portrayed Bérénice had he been called upon to elaborate a Spanish setting around her. One essential quality would have remained, that of alienation from her surroundings. Bérénice is not at home in the marshes of Aigues Mortes, but neither can Barrès make her a native of the harsh, austere city of Toledo. He would have to have her born in Andalusia so that her instinct for color, gaiety and sensuality may be repressed. He would have to make her more passionate, fit to arouse the desires of a man of energy rather than the fickle interest of a torpid Philippe. Instead of fading out of life, a Spanish Bérénice would quit life in a burst of pyrotechnics. Barrès feels that the poetic qualities latent in Bérénice but not given a chance to surface would become more marked in the torrid atmosphere of Toledo. Her basic qualities, tempered by a more violent opposition, would become more clearly marked. True for Bérénice, this is even more true for Barrès. He loves Spain not just for itself, but also because its alien qualities reveal his own true nature to himself.

With this in mind, Barrès returns to the problem of melancholy and concludes that this state is undesirable only when it swamps other feeling. A little melancholy can be a useful tonic to spice up other pleasures. The thought of death can be exciting, because it emphasizes all too fragile youth and beauty. It is Barrès' contention that most sensitive people, after a certain point discover that only death lends a certain spice to their actions. Crises which often appear religious on the surface are simply methods of squeezing the last drop of pleasure out of life. At this stage, Barrès sees this belief as one of the main motives behind Pascal's conversion.

The asceticism of Spain may be explained in the same light. When sheer physical pleasure is exhausted, the mind takes over and finds joy in privation instead of in indulgence. In his summary, Barrès explains Spain's intensity of feeling in terms of its position as an outpost of Europe. Forces which have gradually been eliminated from other countries have found root in Spain and flourished. Contradictions instead of annulling each other, feed on each other until they develop to extremes. Spain's ultimate value is to provide a living example of the dictum which Philippe has already formulated in the *Culte du moi* — when our sentiments are in danger of becoming commonplace, they may be spiced up by mixing them with their opposites to form an intense contrast.

Barrès' attitude towards Italy is quite distinct from his attitude towards Spain. Italy, particularly northern Italy, is further removed from the violent exoticism of Africa and the Middle East. Its charm is perceptible only in small doses. The traveller will enjoy passing through, but will not be tempted to stay. Spain enhances feelings, but Italy suppresses them by drowning them in agreeable trivialities. The self-discipline so dear to Barrès seems to make no sense in this climate of relaxed sensuality which creates dilettantes, and which has come close to captivating Sturel. "Indulgence" is the term appearing most readily under Barrès' pen to describe these regions. The most sordid adventures appear to be endorsed by a certain attraction. Italy at its worst is typified by Ravenna, whose sadness and melancholy drown out all enthusiasm. It forces Barrès to face the rather unpleasant suspicion that he has no real attachment to the passions and enthusiasms he attempts to develop within himself. Not even death can add its accustomed spice to life, as in Spain. Barrès can imagine dying in Ravenna out of sheer boredom, rather than because pushed to its limit the band of life has snapped.

What part has Barrès' own homeland to play, compared to this violent or morbid exoticism? A simple scene, a chance phrase, may awaken his emotions and reverberate through his consciousness. In general his thoughts tend to be grouped around attitudes of altruism. A visit to the zoo reinforces his love of humanity which has been capable of emancipating itself from the blind instinct of self-conservation. The contemplation of human suffering obliges him to recognize its value as a purifying agent. The thought of death awakens his interest in those who might otherwise have passed by unnoticed. A sense of fraternity seems to exude from the animals and the trees. Contact with the richness of others implies for Barrès that we should develop our own richness. Barrès' homeland, though outwardly not so exciting as Spain or Italy brings him back to his true purpose, the development of his own ego as an enlightened representative of his nation.

II   Amori et dolori sacrum

Engrossed in his 1903 political campaign, Barrès paid scant attention to the success of this book,[6] which cast an indulgent glance on a past he had outgrown. The subtitle, "Death of Venice" refers principally to the position the city occupies in his life and thought. Venice, because it has shattered his guard and reached into the inner recesses of his being is both exhilarating and dangerous. It is not so much because, as he later claims, Venice threatens to substitute a foreign culture for that of his native Lorraine. The real danger of Venice is that it will encourage his latent Romanticism.

There are abundant signs that Barrès is still drawn to some of Romanticism's attitudes. His appreciation of the paintings of Tiepolo is based on his conviction that they typify the vaguely defined malady of *épuisement* — a physical and moral exhaustion generally linked with the decadent representatives of a race which has lived too long.[7] He rejoices in the notion that the splendor of Venice conceals a world-weariness which turns ordinary pleasures into dust and ashes. The people whom Venice influences in this way become soul brothers of the exceptional Romantic hero whose talents and sensitivity cause him to spend his life in an ambiguously welcomed isolation.

A further expression of Barrès' Romanticism is his attraction to the themes of decay and dissolution. Youth cannot interest him because it has not yet had time to store up a cultural or emotive heritage. Barrès whether he realizes it or not finds himself in agreement with the decadent who believes that truly appreciable pleasure is to be found only in a civilization on the point of final collapse. The predominance of the notion of death is naturally linked to this idea of refinement *in extremis*. It is also linked with the conviction that pleasure is to be found only in extremes of emotion. The decadent rapidly exhausts normal pleasure and is obliged to have recourse to increasingly unusual sensations to galvanize his jaded senses. Whether he chooses sadism or masochism, death is the limit beyond which he cannot push. The decadent therefore creates a subtle game out of coming as close to death as possible without actually destroying the source of his pleasures.

There still linger other hangovers from Romanticism which will be banished from his later work. The thought of impenitent nuns, for example, who put their sensual pleasures before their vows delights Barrès as it had earlier delighted Stendhal. In *La Colline inspirée* however, Barrès was to censure severely those nuns who put their own interests before the interests of the order represented by the authority of Rome.

On other occasions Barrès despairs that the human mind can create nothing new; and that what appear to be the latest advances in philosophical thought are but restatements, often in similar terms of the conclusions of our ancestors. Barrès will not change his opinion but his attitude will change, and despair turn into a triumphant expression of gratitude that the links with the past are so strongly maintained.

Since the book is to an appreciable extent a work of transition, there are other qualities which denote a development from the attitudes of Romanticism and decadence. His attraction to animality is a case in point. Where the decadent admires energy, it is usually an energy discerned in others; the barbarians who he believes are the forerunners of a new civilization which will sweep away his over-extended culture. As Barrès makes clear in his first trilogy, he has no intention of allowing himself to be swept away by barbarians. When he recognizes energy in others it is because he intends to emulate them and surpass them. Barrès' cult of energy is therefore much more than the feeble admiration of the decadent for an energy which he cannot share. Through animality, Barrès expresses his determination to take raw energy and use it for his own ends. These ends often bear a close relationship to the everyday and the practical which cannot be tolerated by the pure esthete who seeks to isolate himself from the world. Barrès' ventures into politics, even if only to enrich his own personality, betray a willingness to come to grips with society that is quite diferent from the decadent's attempts to shield himself from all mundane contacts.

Espousing this much more practical point of view Barrès can develop a more healthy attitude towards the past. He does not defy the present or yearn for the glories of a bygone age as does Huysmans. He does not waste time regretting the destruction of the past. Instead, he sees the continuation of the past in the present. This in turn modifies his attitude toward modernity which is to be deplored only when it debases the spirit of which it is the latest expression. The past is to be revered, but not necessarily preserved. Decay and death are simply preludes to resurrection. Like the proverbial phoenix rising out of the ashes of its dead self, the present is born from the past.

Man's role in all this is to understand the process as it applies to himself and the world around him. He must dominate his surroundings and not allow himself to be overwhelmed by them. All too often the Romantic allows himself to be overcome by the spectacle of nature. Not so Barrès who rejects nature when it fails to provoke the sensations he requires in favor of humanity. For him nature is always an instrument to be used or put aside at will. Whatever the object of his contemplation, it is not supposed to arouse nostalgia as it does in the Romantic, but rather a deeper understanding of one's own self. At this stage in his thought Barrès has definitely broken with his past and is attempting to allot to Venice a secondary role as a catalyst. Refusing to admit that Venice might have exercised a dangerous spell over him, he claims that it has merely awakened him to the traditional values of his native Lorraine. He goes even further, insinuating that Venice is just another jewel in the crown of Latin civilization of which Lorraine is the primary defender.

Barrès has now reached the point where he can affirm that regardless of his preoccupations of the moment, all lead eventually to nationalism. In saying so he claims to have turned Romanticism into a well defined discipline. Barrès is not exactly anti-romantic. He speaks out against the fumbling Romanticism which seeks sensation for its own sake without attempting to understand the nature of its own inner compulsions. He is too aware of his roots in the past however, to reject Romanticism out of hand. He is not a Zola who despairs of ever extirpating the last traces of the Romantic poison. He takes as his own whatever the past has to offer in the belief that his predecessors have made mistakes so that he might avoid them.

The book is two things at the same time. First, it is an account of Barrès' first impressions of Venice. The general atmosphere of genteel decadence stems from this. Second, the book is the crystallization of fifteen years of reflection on these first impressions from which stems the doctrine which allows him to make sometimes critical judgments of the figures he continues to admire, such as Byron, George Sand, or Gautier.

In summary, Barrès believes that even though Romanticism continues to be the life-style of a good many people, it is none the less moribund. Like all great formative phases of the past, Romanticism should be accorded respect but only a limited role in active life. Nothing is stable. Life is a constant process of development and change. Romanticism becomes most destructive when it is "frozen" and falls out of harmony with the world around it. Its most valuable contribution has been to arouse man's energy and enthusiasm making him realize that there are new possibilities beyond the fixed forms of Classicism. The cult of energy associated with Romanticism has to be preserved and channeled into new forms. If that is done Barrès believes that despair and ennui can be avoided. His own quest for new forms eventually leads him into nationalism which he believes can offer the assurance and stability that Romanticism has lost.

The claim of the title, that the book is dedicated to love and suffering, needs to be explained in the light of Barrès' criticism of Romanticism. The suffering does not reflect the attraction to cruelty that Barrès has encountered in Spain. It is not physical, but the product of unappeased longing. Barrès can admire a person whose tastes are so elevated that he cannot find satisfaction, but he sees no need to make any attempt at emulation. Suffering can be counteracted by love, not just physical love whose effects are momentary but the love which projects a person outside his own selfish interests into an encounter with others. It is love in the sense of respect for others, allied to discipline, which Barrès believes will guarantee a healthy approach to the future.

III   Le Voyage de Sparte

When Barrès travelled through Greece in 1900 he already possessed notions of Classicism gleaned from the ruins of Spain and Italy; from Burdeau; from the eminent Classicist Louis Ménard;

from a young Armenian acquaintance, Tigrane;[8] even from
Goethe.

Armed with this cultural baggage, Barrès nevertheless
approaches Greece with some trepidation. The rounded phrases of
Ménard, so full of meaning in Paris, strike him as hollow when
Barrès is actually standing on the site of the Acropolis. Tigrane has
enthused over the exploits of a modern Greece but has perceived
only the most tenuous links between Greece and its classical past.
When Barrès actually stands on Greek soil he perceives that
Ménard, Tigrane and Goethe are all too close to Western Europe to
be the intermediaries he has imagined them to be. Goethe's Iphi-
geneia with her gentleness and forgiveness is too far removed from
the savagery of the Greek original. European art presents one ideal
of harmony but Barrès suspects that the ancient Greek ideal is a
much more violent and bloody one. The almost immediate contradiction of his previously formed opinions leads to a feeling of dis-
orientation accompanied by hesitation and misgiving. Even at the
outset he has begun to regret his journey into the unknown when he
could have been revisiting the Spain or Italy he already has tamed.
He seeks to cling to the familiar by thinking of the familiar figures
who have preceded him. In the end however, the cultural shock of
Greece proves too violent. Rather than relying on the interpretations of others he is forced to come to terms with Greece in his own
way and derive his own lessons.

Barrès now attempts to forge a Greece that he can understand. A
major concern is to show that the so-called classical ideal of a universal reason applicable to all mankind is merely a myth created by
Anaxagoras and Phidias, two old style counterparts of modern
internationally minded humanists who are out of touch with the
majority of the people. What is known as Hellenism thus becomes
the doctrine of a small, uprooted elite which has lost touch with
popular traditions.

To gain a clearer understanding of what these traditions are,
Barrès abandons Phidias and turns to Antigone. She appeals above
all to his sense of continuity. By her charity and her piety she reminds him of modern nuns whose prayers redeem the sins of
others. By her love for her brothers she reminds him of the goddess
Rosmertha, worshipped with her brother by the Celtic pagans who
once inhabited the Moselle valley. Most important, however, she
embodies the determination to maintain harmony by fulfilling the

old traditions even in the face of overwhelming obstacles. Before he can fully admire Antigone, however, Barrès has to deal with one tricky problem. Creon represents the voice of authority which Barrès is always inclined to respect if it is legitimately constituted. No matter how heroic and virtuous Antigone may be, she is only a mere disturber of the social order if Creon's authority is justified. After some discussion Barrès eventually decides to yield to his admiration for Antigone. His imagination persuades him that the real villain of the affair is Tiresias who seeks to draw power to himself while using Creon as an unwitting pawn. It is Tiresias who brings about Antigone's death and Creon's abdication the better to consolidate his own rule through their weak successors. Antigone thus becomes the victim of an opportunist who rejects the popular traditions made up of piety towards both the living and the dead, respect for the hallowed symbols of authority and a harmonious adjustment of the present to the past. Barrès feels closer to the amorphous mass of long forgotten people than to their so-called representatives.

Barrès attempts to link this half-buried popular sentiment with the French spirit which has bubbled forth and spread out across the East at the time of the Crusades. He claims that these armies, like the revolutionary armies of Napoleon after them, have come to liberate the oppressed and proclaim the rights of freedom. In these final pages Barrès begins to show the enthusiasm for cultural colonization that he is to express so forcefully almost twenty years later in *Une enquête aux pays du Levant*. Dwelling on the rapid French expansion in the past cannot but raise the problem of why this outburst of energy has suddenly dried up as rapidly as it had appeared. Remembering 1870, Barrès is afraid that even at the height of their powers the French were afflicted with a failure complex. The problem of expressing energy and creativity is posed as he witnesses a local traditional dance. Dances, for Barrès, are generally associated with a return to the springs of mystic energy; but this dance appears so grave, calm and stylized that no inspiration from it is possible.

As often when the facts do not completely fit, Barrès has recourse to his imagination. The legend of Pegasus and Bellerophon seems to contain the elements necessary to an understanding of the Greek expression of energy. He claims that the artificial reason of the small elite who had built the Parthenon was incapable of expressing the unconscious impulse which stirred in the collective

Greek soul. The Parthenon builders sought to extend their domination over the unconscious, whereas Pegasus and Bellerophon form a harmonious unity in which neither side dominates. Pegasus is the creative spirit, always running the risk of attaining such rarified heights that the limits of insanity and solitude are reached. Bellerophon is the control who channels this creative energy, not by force of reason, but by love and understanding. Here Barrès feels he has grasped the secret of the successful application of energy. It will peter out if used purely to dominate others but increase if used to form partnership and communion with others. The task of the controller is a very delicate one. Too much control will lead to the stifling of the creative impulse. Too little control will lead to the stifling of the control itself. Barrès mind harks back again to the fate of the French crusaders. They had settled down and their union with the local population produced the Gasmules. In other terms the fusion of the two energies, foreign and local, created an outstanding type of woman in whom were blended the best features of the French and the Greek. Then the French, seduced by their own creation, allow themselves to give way to it. Their control is lost and without it they lose the major distinguishing feature of their Frenchness, sense of honor and sense of action.

When Barrès contemplates with dismay the possibility that his ego will be entrapped and his energy drained off into the voluptuous resignation of the Orient, he all too often reacts with a regression into savagery and cruelty. "Man is not meant to dream," he says, "but to bite and to savage."[9] The man who ignores the struggle of everyday existence the better to concentrate on the development of his ego and his inner energies does so at his peril. Barrès is now ready for his arrival in Sparta which has been fully conscious of the necessity for strength and power. His desire to discover a strong antidote to what he is aware is an all too dangerous receptivity to melancholy and sensuality explains his temporary enthusiasm for Spartan cruelty. More lasting is his enthusiasm for the Spartan form of nationalism which represses the misdirected development of individuality in favor of the development of nobility in the collectivity. Glory and action are the keynotes of the Spartan state but they are linked to a sense of rootedness in the land from which they draw their strength. In the long run therefore, the Spartans also express that mystic harmony stemming from a sense of unity which is also Barrès' long sought goal.

Upon his return from Greece in 1900, Barrès did not quite know what to make of what he had seen. The lessons of the land seemed to be complex and contradictory. He was not even sure whether they applied to him or not. Then in 1903 he met Anna de Noailles who seemed so much to personify the contradictions of the land of her origins. She is the figure behind the portraits of the Gasmules whose beauty, sensitivity and sensuality enslave future generations of would-be French conquerors. The contradictions which had once been abstract, now became real for Barrès, a part of his living experience with which he could deal. The account of his journey to Greece was completed two years after his encounter with Mme de Noailles. Barrès' first concern is to distinguish between an artificial Greece which is nothing but the creation of a cosmopolitan elite of abstract humanist thinkers and the real Greece of the people. This Greece is a perfect, harmonious union of action and revery, energy and sensuality, realism and poetry.

The drawback is that Barrès risks being overwhelmed by the very perfection of the vision. He feels himself to be diminished, while the previous influence of Venice, Seville or Toledo becomes all but obliterated. When confronted with the danger of being absorbed, Barrès always reacts by drawing upon his Lorraine origins. He admits to his intellectual admiration for Greek perfection, but does not necessarily accept it as his own kind of perfection. He may recognize the Greek ideal as a shining example of what can be attained, but he claims that he has to reach the goal in his own way without denying any of the elements of his culture. Above all, the Greek ideal is dormant. It belongs to the past not to the present. Its role is to provide encouragement. Both France and Greece are countries which, after suffering humiliation and defeat, are poised on the brink of a great spiritual renascence. War has not only cleansed and purified them. It has also forced them to take account of elements from the outside which are vitally important to stimulate a nation out of the attempt to perpetuate a static image of itself without allowing for growth and development. In the name of the old ideal, Barrès expects that both France and Greece can progress to even greater heights.

IV   Greco ou Le Secret de Tolède

For centuries after his death El Greco's works gathered dust in the churches of Toledo, unlooked at and uncared for. All too often, when Barrès expresses the desire to see the paintings, he is told by the locals that it is not worth the trouble, that they are the work of a demented man. They are sold at ridiculously low prices and even given away as part of election campaign deals. Although some scholars are beginning to take some interest in this painter, and the task of tracing and cataloguing his work is well under way, Barrès is one of the first writers to attempt a popular study, and to explain in comprehensive terms the wayward genius of this foreigner in the land of Spain. It is something of a surprise that Barrès should even want to study such a figure. Born it is thought, on the island of Crete, El Greco follows many of his contemporaries to Venice, a thriving city of the arts made glorious by Titian and Tintoretto. It is here that El Greco develops the traditional skills of form and color before coming to settle in Toledo. From this short sketch we expect El Greco to be a typical uprooted man, deprived of his old culture without being able to assimilate the culture of his new background. It is not apparently so. El Greco is one of those rare figures who succeeds in achieving continual enrichment without sacrificing his native genius.[10]

Barrès' attachment to El Greco is a prolongation of the temptations of Orientalism. The city of Toledo takes on a new dimension as the adopted city of this complex painter. Long known for its austere Catholicism, it is also the home of large numbers of Arabs and Jews whose attachment to Christianity is token at best. Although the Inquisition is never able to eradicate them completely, it does succeed in reducing their influence to the point of being in modern times, a merely titillating but not dangerous novelty. Barrès' thoroughgoing approval of the massacres carried out in the name of racial and religious purity betrays the unconscious desire to treat his opponents in the same way. His description of modern vestiges of Orientalism, full of strongly sensuous terms suggests the desire of the victor to ravish the vanquished and thus ratify his conquest. The danger of Orientalism disappears when it is possessed in this way by the brutal conqueror reveling in his strength. Barrès is able to yield to the temptations of Orientalism when he is sure that they cannot overcome the duties of nationalism.

In his study of the painter, Barrès adopts the standpoint of the sensitive man, rather than that of the scholar. In doing so, he is true to his conviction that deep emotion is closer to truth than the spirit of intellectualism. He prefers not to undertake a technical study but seeks to describe his own reactions in the belief that these will truly reflect the hidden intentions of the artist in question. Any student of El Greco's work is immediately faced with the strong contrast between reality and the imagination. His best known work is characterized by elongated, distorted figures which often seem to create lines of force emanating outwards towards the periphery of the canvas. Attempts have been made to ascribe this style to astigmatism on the painter's part, but this rather specious argument collapses in view of the perfectly normal, minutely detailed figures that he is able to produce at the same time.

Barrès explanation is by far the better one. He presents El Greco as a talented craftsman who has gained fluent mastery over the technical aspects of his profession during apprenticeship in Venice. When he is not moved and captivated by his subject, he renders it neatly and exactly as he has been taught to do. When a subject fires his imagination, however, the effort to express his own striving for perfection results in the swirl of movement associated with his distinctive style.

The strong sense of disquiet projected by these paintings is according to Barrès, perhaps due to the attempt to reconcile contradictory elements in El Greco's own nature. The modern Greek writer Kazantzakis, himself born on Crete, claims that there is a streak of independence and toughness in the Cretan character that refuses to be subdued. Subject to the contradictory influences of Hellenism, Islam and Catholicism, El Greco strives to express his own individuality. It is because he is a man of many cultures that El Greco succeeds best in expressing the spirit of Toledo, a city of many cultures.

In retrospect the book is an important milestone in the development of Barrès' attitudes. The strange mixture of Arab and Christian themes prefigure one of the major themes of *Un Jardin sur l'Oronte* and the preoccupation with the expression of mysticism and energy is to increase as the need to strengthen France against Germany grows pressing. Last, but by no means least, Barrès proves to be a remarkably sensitive artist himself, capable of a delicacy which he cannot allow himself to express on all occasions.

CHAPTER 8

Mysticism

D ESPITE the comfort he has gained from religious services as a
lonely schoolboy, Barrès adopts the popular attitude among
adolescents of scorn for organized religion. Like Diderot, he
assumes that Catholicism exists only for old people who, when they
can sin no more are able to use forgiveness wisely.[1] As a socialist he
denounces clericalism and its attempts to cash in on the Socialist
movement.[2] He cruelly mocks Sarcey for defending the very teaching orders in the Middle East that he himself will help to re-
establish some thirty-five years later.[3] In a sense, Barrès is never
reconciled with Catholicism as a dogma. His last recorded profession of faith shows that while he feels himself at one with Christ,
for the Church,[4] he feels love and admiration but not belief.

His interest in religion is aroused when he realizes that man is
molded by more than materialistic powers. First he attempts to link
the forces of mysticism with Socialism[5] while denouncing the pure
materialism of Marxism. In *L'Ennemi des lois* Barrès affirms that
spiritual force expresses itself through love. His conviction is confirmed by Abbé Brémond,[6] (whom he meets in the course of his trip
through Greece) and finds its way into *La Colline inspirée*. Lastly,
Barrès appreciates Catholicism because it is monotheistic in name
only, and continues to encourage the pluralistic worship of the
pagan gods in the guise of saints.[7] He appreciates Catholicism as
much for its preservation of pagan tradition as for its control of
mystic energies. Pope Pius XI was quite justified in claiming Barrès
as one of the Church's defenders on the outside.[8]

I   La Grande Pitié des Eglises de France

This book presents a summary of Barrès' efforts on behalf of
the churches of France, threatened with neglect and disrepair

because of the curious circumstances attached to the separation of church and state. His first serious move, an open letter addressed to Briand, leads to a meeting between the two at which each attempts to press his point of view. Barrès seems to refrain from fully developing his deepest convictions on the matter. He confines himself to the need for repair without indicating what role he believes the churches can play in the life of the nation. As a result his conversation with Briand is fraught with misunderstanding. He does little to dissipate the misunderstanding in his first speech in January 1911 when he uses the discussion of the budget for interior affairs as a pretext for bringing the plight of the churches to public attention. He speaks of the artistic value of the churches but he fails to show clearly how he links his preoccupation to his concern with the survival of the church as a spiritual force. His conclusion that the upkeep of the churches is a national affair cannot be made with the full force he intends.

Despite his initial lack of success, Barrès begins to gain support among the general public. Encouraged by this groundswell of favorable opinion Barrès determines to bring up the matter again in the Chamber. He suggests quite simply that all churches built before 1800 be automatically classified as national monuments. The state is then expected to play a major role in repairing them by absorbing most of the costs. The proposal is defended in a lively speech by his Socialist friend, Sembat. When Beauquier, an avowed anti-clerical rises to make his usual point that God refuses to perform any miracles on His churches' behalf, Sembat replies that if Beauquier were a monument, Barrès would certainly propose that he be preserved for the archaic quality of his thought. Despite Sembat's support, Barrès knows that the vote will be close. When the results are announced he is some two dozen votes short. He feels that his proposal has been killed by the insinuation that he is attempting to re-establish the responsibility of the state to finance religion, not just repair the buildings in which religion is practised.

About four months later in March 1913, Barrès feels called upon to make a third speech, adding to his original proposal suggestions that will amount to the creation of private funds to be administered by the bishops of the dioceses. Unfortunately, a proliferation of amendments and subamendments creates an atmosphere of confusion and Barrès is defeated again. From this point on, his energies are channeled in other directions by the intervention of the war and by his reports in favor of the reestablishment of teaching orders on French soil. He does not, however, forget his devotion to the French churches and occasionally in his articles for the *Echo de Paris,* mentions their participation in French suffering when they endure the bombardment of German barbarism.[9]

His opponents often accused Barrès of being too interested in reestablishing the rights of an already overly powerful Catholic church. They considered his defense of the archeological and artistic value of local churches a screen for his real intentions. In a way they are correct, although they totally misunderstand what his real intentions are. For Barrès, the wood and stone of the churches has no intrinsic value. They are simply symbols of a greater idea. It would be mechanically feasible to remove statues or stained glass windows or other examples of architectural art and put them on display in a clean, readily accessible museum. In such a setting they would lose all their evocative value. All their power stems from their local surroundings. The strength of these local influences is apparent to Barrès by the discovery that even when the local squire calls in artists and builders from Paris, they create works in the spirit of the local traditions, adding only the grace and power of their craftsmanship. It is wrong, therefore, to choose to preserve only outstanding examples of a given school or period. What matters to Barrès are the subtle variations from the norm indicative of a powerful local instinct. More than any other buildings, Barrès believes, churches are the guardians and transmitters of this local spirit. To destroy them is to destroy a cultural heritage. His theories of uprootedness come into play here. In a strange museum, objects lose their soul. In their own setting, however, they continue as living, growing things.

The question still remains in the minds of his opponents: what is the value for modern man in the cultural heritage these objects represent? His critics remember the church's opposition to the development of scientific enquiry, and its unfortunate alliance with the aristocracy of the *ancien régime* to oppress the people. Barrès attempts to avoid setting one faction against another. He sees science and religion not as enemies, but equally important elements in the human situation.[10] He is just as willing to campaign in favor of scientific progress as for the preservation of churches. Rather than diminishing his cultural heritage by favoring one above the other, he prefers to try and ally the rationalism of science with the mystic impulse of faith. Neither one can alone maintain a human being at a high level of civilization. If the influence of the church is diminished, rationalism will not take over and fill the gap. Religion fulfills certain spiritual needs which cannot be met by the public school. Given the persistence of the religious longing in mankind it becomes a question, not of destroying religion, but of choosing which religion to be influenced by.

As far as Barrès is concerned, there are two major possibilities for the majority of Frenchmen: a return to a violent, primitive paganism; or an acceptance of modern Catholicism. He discounts totally the possibility of a "new" religion such as Auguste Comte or Emile Zola have attempted to establish. He does not deny the sincerity of those who believe in the need for a new religion. He simply believes that the task is far too long and complicated, and that in the meantime it is safer to rely on the proven organization of the church.

The church controls not just by repression, but by giving direction. It channels man's spiritual energies to constructive ends and prevents them from destroying him. Its two thousand years of experience cannot easily be replaced by a new, untried institution. Barrès brings a keenly felt personal experience to the argument. As a young man he had sought to affirm his personality through battle. Faced with phenomena foreign to his personality, his instinctive reaction had been to struggle with them, not to destroy them, but to wrest from them their secret. Without fully realizing it at the time, he had been close to the old pagan attitude of absorbing the virtue of one's enemies through conquest and assimilation. As he grew older, Barrès had come to understand that while this manner might enable him to experience new ideas and sensations, it was failing to develop the mysterious forces which had been present since his birth at the root of his personality. The church had long since realized that personal struggle was ultimately self-defeating and that one's personality could better be developed to a high pitch through harmony and understanding.

In a museum, contemplating a twenty thousand year old representative of Homo Sapiens discovered in a cave near Menton, Barrès allows his imagination to reconstruct what his thoughts must have been when this pre-civilization man struggled for existence in a hostile environment. Ten years later these questions were still turning over in Barrès' mind. It had been his intention to develop them in a book but all that we possess of them are some fragments under the heading *L'Homme préhistorique.*[11] Man takes his first stride towards full self-development with the realization that he is doomed to die, says Barrès.[12] The inevitability of death leads to anguish, but also to curiosity; the desire to know and understand brings our human destiny into the light. Man creates religion as a consolation and tool of discovery. Crude and barbaric at first, religions gradually become more refined and more adept at assuaging man's spiritual needs. Barrès sincerely believes that the highest form of religious expression is Catholicism. Science can collaborate with religion, but not replace it. Science is the indispensable tool for the observation of the physical world, but out of its element in dealing with spiritual matters.

In his youth Barrès had been all too familiar with colleagues who have the utmost belief in the capacity of science to answer the riddle of man's destiny and who have fallen into a despairing nihilism when science uncovers more mysteries than it can solve. It does not matter that science should in its nature be materialistic — provided that man does not rely on science alone. When he does, the results are plain to see. He disfigures the earth, pours chemical wastes into the rivers, chokes the valleys with slag heaps, and stifles the mysterious, poetic intuition of man in a covering of poisonous filth.

The destroyers, contemptuous of man's finer instincts are the brothers of those who seek to destroy the churches and prevent all people from experiencing the uplifting virtue of religion because they are incapable of experiencing it themselves. For this same reason, Barrès refuses to allow the churches to be reduced to the role of market places or political forums. The church is a living, growing body, extending its civilizing influence to the whole of the nation. It is not enough for just the Catholics to maintain the churches. Everyone has to do so in order to participate in its benefits. Civilization Barrès believes, depends on the harmonious development of science and religion. In defending the churches, Barrès feels that he is defending an integral part of France.

II   La Colline inspirée

This account undergoes a long process of maturation before its eventual publication in 1913. Léopold is first mentioned in the *Cahiers* in 1902, while in 1906 and 1907 Barrès sketches out the major themes of the novel together with plans to link them with appropriate episodes.[13] Once he has decided what his general attitude is to be be Barrès feels able to confront the piles of documents related to the history of the Baillard brothers and sort out the elements he needs.[14] Barrès makes his approach clear in the first chapter in which his major preoccupation is with the hill of Sion-Vaudémont itself. The hill has a value all its own. It is a magical place, having served as a sanctuary for the pagan gods before being christianized by the construction of a chapel. Into this setting step the three Baillard brothers: Quirin, François and their leader Léopold, the eldest. The story Barrès writes is largely the story of Léopold and of his dialogue with the forces of the hill.

Léopold is born in 1796 when the worst of the revolutionary terror is still a living fact. He is an example of Barrès' belief that a great individual does not appear suddenly but is formed by a long line of more or less obscure ancestors. His family is noted for its fervor and for its protection of fugitive priests during the revolution; one member has baptized Léopold and predicted an outstanding career for him. Léopold's first act on leaving the seminary is to revive a defunct Benedictine convent with such success that the institution rapidly prospers. He sees himself as a new spiritual leader, and so the better to prepare himself for his task, plunges himself into the study of the life and teachings of the great founders of spiritual orders, including the local hero, Saint Pierre Fourier. Barrès imagines that Léopold already envisages himself as having, not just a general duty to the Church, but a special duty to Lorraine in addition. He falls under the influence of a group of scholars who believe like Barrès that Lorraine has a special role to play in taming the energies of barbarianism and using them to promote enlightened civilization. He sets about buying up the land and the ruins on the hill of Sion, determined to raise there a symbol of Lorraine and Christian power.

Although Léopold is motivated by such exalted sentiments Barrès does not forget to underscore that Léopold retains his peasant mentality. He possesses the practical genius of a Santa Teresa but not the utter obedience which has enabled her to submit herself to the orders of her hierarchical superiors.[15] Barrès gives proof of a rather ambiguous attitude towards the growing opposition to the Baillards within the church. On the one hand the church represents order and obedience imposed on the ebullient forces of mysticism when they threaten to run out of control. On the other hand the hierarchical authorities are themselves tainted with unworthy motives. The church is an international organization and the authorized representative of the Pope who has come to judge Léopold and his convent cannot but look with suspicion on the creator of an institution so strongly rooted in a sense of local pride. The fierce sense of injustice Léopold experiences is understandable. In the long run however, Barrès' love of order overcomes his local prejudices and he agrees that the Baillards' disgrace, their enforced resignation from the institutions they have developed is both necessary and merited.

To cool their ardor somewhat, the three brothers are ordered to spend thirty days in the calm and tranquility of a Carthusian monastery. The atmosphere affects them in ways different according to their individual temperaments. Léopold sets up barriers against the outside world and turns his thoughts inward. Naturally enough he finds no peace of mind and is in a sufficiently exalted state to accept as divine guidance the rather imprudent suggestion of one of the monks that he call on Vintras.

Although the second half of the nineteenth century is generally thought of as an age devoted to positivism and scientific materialism, a grass roots religious fervor developed and resulted in some astonishing phenomena and outrageous claims. Eugène Vintras was the rather mediocre bastard child of a poor peasant girl, until the Archangel Michael revealed him to be the reincarnation of the prophet Elisha. He founded the "Carmel," a new church with a new priesthood destined to replace the corrupt, worldly priesthood of the Catholic church.

Having suffered at his superiors' hands, Léopold is naturally ready to embrace a doctrine which guarantees him revenge. After two weeks spent with Vintras, Léopold encourages his brothers to join him. They all return to Lorraine full of enthusiasm for the new doctrine and ready to create a new church to overthrow the old one.

Although welcome at first they are soon rejected by the populace. Barrès ascribes the change to the peasants' instinctive good sense and their rejection of anarchy. We know that for Barrès, anarchy means excessive individualism and the disorders it entails. To the peasant mind, disorderly conduct is most apparent in the cohabitation of monks and nuns. Barrès more than once describes the nuns as witches; and there can be no doubt that among their demonic attributes, he means to hint at sexual disorders. Anarchy is also to be blamed for distorting the mystic impulse. Léopold relies too much on himself. Confronted with the problem of self-development, Léopold has thought foremost of his own satisfaction. The institutions he has founded have been intended primarily to assuage his pride and to bring him glory. He has attempted to keep all the credit for himself instead of turning it over to the church. When the church understandably expels him and he is cut off from its guidance, he naturally becomes more wrapped up in his desire for vengeance — to the extent that he welcomes the invasion of France by Prussia as a divine sign that he is justified. If further proof is needed of his disastrous self-reliance it lies in his attitude towards the Virgin, which is that of the sorcerer who makes the higher powers do his bidding either through force or through gratitude.

Despite Léopold's fundamental error, there is much to be admired in him. Barrès dislikes the pettiness of Léopold's enemies, who he feels could use a little of Léopold's enthusiasm. The brothers with their ceremonies, succeed for a moment in spiritualizing the peasants and making them forget their material occupations, something that the official church has not succeeded in doing. Ideally the church should be aware of the mystic impulse and attempt to guide it for the individual's self-fulfillment. All too often, however, the church is afraid and attempts instead to crush it. A further point in Léopold's favor is that he is to some extent a defender of native forces against Rome. Barrès never actually regards Rome as an invader. He speaks consistently of a Western Christian civilization of which France is an integral part; indeed, the leading integral part. The local forces need to fall under the harmonizing influence represented by the Church. Barrès criticizes the church only when, instead of promoting the natural development of local forces it seeks to suppress them in the name of order. Barrès is normally fully in favor of order and control,[16] and he greatly admires the church's power of organization, if only for its efficiency. The loss of this organization, as in the nuns' case, leads to manifestations of uprootedness. No longer of the peasant class but also no longer of the church, they lack the discipline whch can smooth over their internal rivalries. Yet order, without love and understanding is sterile and repressive. The visiting Abbé Florentin reminds the reader of one of Diderot's automatons. Confronted

with anything that differs slightly from orthodox doctrine, Florentin automatically labels it "satanism" without considering that
something of value might lie behind it.

Whatever the rights and wrongs of the affair the Baillard's are
defeated. To support themselves and their few remaining followers
they have to take on backbreaking manual labor. In spite of this
hard life Léopold becomes more and more spiritualized as he drifts
further away from reality. He no longer dreams of perpetuating his
name in institutions of brick and mortar but only of liberating the
poetry of his soul. He becomes more responsive to the magic of the
elements, cutting himself off completely from social and religious
order. It is in lack of discipline that he differs from great artists —
Barrès mentions Beethoven and Milton — who produce some of
their most exciting work when physical disabilities cut them off
from reality.

Léopold's new sensitivity however, serves him well on occasions
when the church representatives prove coarse and unimaginative.
In the course of excavations for the foundations of a new building
on the site of the hill, workers discover a hermaphrodite statue of
the old religion. In his imagination, Léopold joins with the forgotten priest who has reverently hidden the holy relic and understands something about the mixed religious fervor and despair
which has filled him. The priests less sensitive merely regard the
statue as an abomination. Nonetheless, they take it into the church,
unwittingly making the church — perhaps in spite of itself — the
guardian of the spirit of the old almost forgotten traditions.[17] Léopold may be extravagant, but when the priests watch him absorbed
in meditation on the hillside they are themselves forced to consider
supernatural forces and become aware of their own role as active
participants in a holy mystery, not just as defenders of the faith.

Certainly, in the long run, Léopold affects Father Aubry. When
he first arrives, Father Aubry is rather brutal and rigid in his doctrines. Because he has been incapable of understanding or appre-
ciating François, he is unable to obtain François' retraction, and
that worthy man dies excommunicated and impenitent. Now, as he
understands more of Léopold's mystic aspirations, Father Aubry
realizes that had he shown sympathy and love, he might have been
able to bend the brothers' energies to positive works for the good of
the church. But it is too late. Father Aubry is dying and has time
only to consider the good of Léopold's soul. This is the way to Léo-

pold's heart. Father Cléach, instructed by Father Aubry, has the satisfaction of giving Léopold absolution.

Barrès' conclusions frame the story of the Baillard brothers in the first and last chapters. They fall into two categories, human and cultural. The human level conclusion is that man needs constantly to strive for what Barrès calls mystic or religious aspirations. Barrès has nothing but contempt for the "dead" souls who never think of reaching out to develop their inner spiritual resources. This inner development must be accompanied, however, by order and harmony. The church is not necessarily the only guarantee of order and harmony but it is the best one available to the French. Within it one can be sure that the mystic forces will not degenerate into egoism and disunity. The cultural level conclusion is that Celtic and Lorraine civilizations play the same role as the church, filtering out all that is barbaric, that is to say unharmonious and destructive from the Germanic influences. The book is a call for the union of the church with French nationalism. French priests have the opportunity of reinstating the tradition of mystic energy against the crass materialism of Germany. Although written just before the First World War, *La Colline inspirée* looks forward to Barrès' postwar preoccupations with French civilizing influences in the Rhineland and elsewhere.

III   Les Maîtres

When Barrès is given the opportunity to express his abiding interest in Dante he makes it quite clear that his approach to this form of criticism is not a scholarly, impersonal approach but a form of dialogue with Dante's work to see what light may be shed on Dante's deepest preoccupations. Every great work, Barrès thinks, enfolds a lesson appropriate to the needs of successive generations. He envisages Dante as an intermediary between two different types of thought, not just the classical and the Christian, but also, like in a personified Alsace-Lorraine, between the East and the West. Arabic legends are found in Dante's work transformed by limpid Mediterranean light into Christian poetry. A further example of the problems ever present to Barrès' mind is aspiration to greatness. What is it that makes one man superior to his fellows, and how can this thing be encouraged? How can the example of a great writer of the past improve modern man? Barrès develops his thought uneasily at first, trapped by the dilemma that greatness can be developed if one has the potential, but the potential cannot be acquired if it is not already there.

As a superior creator Dante is everything that the majority of so-called artists are not. He does not fall into the trap of art for art's sake which leads to the decadence and dilettantism of the late nineteenth century "fin de siècle," or to the exacerbated anguish of Flaubert. Dante also escapes producing utilitarian art as a form of reaction to art for art's sake. His work is intuitive but not instinctive. Activity, order and emotion are at the very center of his poem yet are unified by a singleness of aim which brings harmony and unity. Barrès digresses briefly to evoke the Romantics whose work suffers from spiritual anarchy and who now lay claim to his interest only through their efforts to discipline themselves. Dante's discipline, on the other hand, does not need to be imposed, but flows outwards from the very core of his being. The purposeless action of the Romantics is futile, a bad example at best, but Dante's action is a living, growing lesson.

Unity is Dante's key theme, a unity which gradually develops outwards to become all-embracing. Three types of unity underscore Dante's work — his personal unity, that harmony of knowledge and spirit which Barrès has already admired; national unity, exploited centuries later by the founders of the Italian nation; and unity of the whole human race. Barrès sees love as the force which will breathe the spark of life into the ideal of universal harmony. When he speaks of love Barrès has in mind the pre-eminence of woman in this field. He feels it significant that Beatrice takes over from Vergil in guiding Dante through Paradise. Through her inspiration, Dante's poetry encompasses the universal. Barrès' admiration for Beatrice here recalls the importance that Philippe gives to Bérénice, or that Guillaume will give to Oriante.

If Barrès had ended his talk here he would have shown himself to be a worthy disciple of the Dante he evokes. Unfortunately his conclusion makes it obvious that for him, unity of the whole human race means the pre-eminence of those cultures of mainly Catholic persuasion. Instead of calling to all men, Dante becomes simply a cornerstone in Barrès' wall to block the encroachments of Germanism. In the end, Barrès' preoccupation with the problems of the Rhineland submerges his interest in wider human problems.

Although at first glance she appears to be quite a different type,

Santa Teresa proves amenable to fostering similar conjectures to
Dante. Like him, she is a curious mixture of the spiritual and the
practical. Her clear grasp of the smallest details of running a convent seem to enhance her mystic energy. Through her actions she
attempts to join her soul with God. Despite Barrès' admiration
there is a point beyond which her lessons fail to reach him.
Although Barrès can admire the combination of her vitality and
earthiness with mysticism, he cannot understand how it is achieved.
The intelligence is powerless to grasp this mystery. It may be experienced but there is no guarantee that it will. Mysticism is dependent upon the grace of God. Systems of exercise and meditation are
merely the remaining shell after the spontaneity infusing them has
been exhausted. Adhering to all the tenets of the system may enable
an individual to achieve a state in which he is ready to receive grace,
but it does not guarantee that grace will be given. Santa Teresa is
useful mainly as an example to encourage us to try to realize our
own potential.

Barrès' third example brings him closer to home. Italy and Spain
possess cultural links with France, but Pascal is a man of French
soil, rooted in Auvergne, the very center of the nation. Barrès finds
in Pascal many of the typical signs of genius that he has described
elsewhere. Pascal achieves, for example, a total harmony between
the material and the spiritual. All the same, something within
Pascal cannot be satisfied. Like Dante, his need for the absolute is
partly inspired by love of a woman, in this case his admiration and
ambition for his sister. Lastly, there is within him that universality
and unity which is the mark of all great men. In Pascal, the Orient
and the Occident meet and fuse to produce something characteristic
of France and also of the human race.

Barrès succeeds in arousing our admiration and enthusiasm when
he confines himself to affirmations of a general nature. As a stylist
Barrès shares something of the magic of Dante. He can evoke the
presence of mystical experience but when he tries to explain it, his
reasoning falls flat. He falls into this trap in his talk on Pascal's
anguish. Barrès' arguments are ill chosen to support his views and
tend to leave the reader with a feeling of antipathy for Pascal,
rather than admiration. Pascal appears as an example of a coward
who rejects the world out of fear. In the name of a selfish, illusory
happiness he cuts himself off from reality and from his fellow-man.
There is a lesson to be learned from comparing Pascal to Goethe.

The latter seeks to perfect himself through developing a love for all
that is beautiful and noble in life but the more presumptuous
Pascal rejects what life has to offer. In his evocation of Pascal,
Barrès fails to achieve the effect he has sought which is to quiet
readers' critical spirit and fire their imagination.[18]

IV   Le Mystère en pleine lumière

This collection had been prepared for publication by Barrès
before his death. With a great deal of mastery he again deals with
the problem of evoking the unity of the human spirit. The subject
of the first essay, the Sibyll of Auxerre is a typical example of how
Barrès can seize upon a seemingly commonplace occurrence or
object and invest it with profound meaning. The Sibyll is a pagan
statue which somehow became incorporated into the architecture
of the cathedral at Auxerre. For Barrès, for whom French Catholic
culture is in large part a continuation of Gallo-Roman paganism,
this event is significant enough in itself. In addition, as if to reinforce the continuity and harmony, Barrès sees a pigeon, symbol of
the Holy Ghost, in apparent conversation with the discredited
prophetess. Why has the Sibyll been given shelter in the church,
and what might be her contribution to Christians? She can
reacquaint them with the sources of prophetic power and inspiration. Above all, she perhaps has something to teach about how to
harness these forces and how to provoke them. She is valuable in
that she offers the promise that her "divine folly," buried for too
long by the repressive "wisdom" of the church will once more be
liberated and developed. She is sheltered in the church for this very
reason, to encourage us to make contact with the forces of heaven,
Barrès suggests.

A series of short passages adds some precise qualifications to the
form that suitable contact with supernatural powers should take.
The first is a warning against the desire to know — one which
Pascal might have done well to heed. Enjoyment and satisfaction
always contain an irreducible element of mystery. If we can experience this mystery in human love, then we are close to experiencing
the divine. On the other hand, the element of mystery should not be
confused with ignorance. Real mysticism is sober, pure, controlled
or, as Barrès puts it, full of light. The touchstone of mystic experience is its essential simplicity. It leaves behind an aura of good-

ness. There are forces of light and forces of darkness. Barrès strives
to develop only the former.

The forces of goodness seem to have a predilection for specific
forms. They inhabit the dove, the robin, the nightingale or the rose.
Barrès is prone to see symbols and augers. A pigeon in his study
becomes a sign of encouragement in his struggle to convey his feelings in words. Women, while they may symbolize the forces of
light, may just as well symbolize the forces of darkness. The princess Ling, like the Queen of Sheba, is determined to prove her own
greatness by enslaving the acknowledged conqueror of her age.
Both of them are aided by their victims themselves, who seem to
possess a desire effectively akin to a death wish. Duke Phing
chooses his own destruction out of the desire to know. His own
musician attempts to dissuade him, realizing that as a man of
action, his master is not capable of withstanding the melancholy
truth stripped of all illusion. The Duke refuses to listen and gives
the order to play the melodies which will pour poison into his soul.
He dies a commonplace death in a fire, but his spiritual death pre-
cedes the fire. The Duke has attempted, like the mystic, to link himself with supernatural forces and participate in their energy. He
succeeds, but realizes too late that he has chosen the wrong type of
force.

Joan of Arc, burned for being a witch is nonetheless a representative of the forces of light. Barrès calls for her intercession during the darkest days of the war,[19] and when it is over, calls again
upon her civilizing influences to protect France from the invasion
of the barbaric hordes to the East.[20] Joan carries to a high degree
the qualities which Barrès believes most important in mysticism —
clarity and simplicity. She is obviously influenced by local forces,
but transforms them. She purifies all the malevolence implicit in
these pagan forces, uniting them with Christianity in a luminous
harmony. She is another Beatrice, and a glorious answer to the dis-
turbing powers of princess Ling. Unlike the latter, who loves only
her own glory, Joan of Arc exhibits perfect love of humanity.

A question which Barrès skirts very delicately is how to distinguish the good from the bad. In the case of Saint Joan, one has to
wait hundreds of years after the event to be sure. Barrès' final conclusions lend an extension to his theory of self-development which
should not be undertaken out of selfishness or superficial motives.
One of the worst examples of self-development is afforded by the

spoiled young brat of "Le Frein couvert d'écume"[21] who progresses from one new sensation to another at the expense of everyone around her. By making herself the center of the world she is effectively a nihilist. When young and pretty, such a woman can disguise her true nature. As age fades her beauty however, "the glittering fairy" reveals herself a destructive sorceress. Self-development must be accompanied by love and respect for others enabling the individual to tap the energies resident in the universal harmony of all humanity. There are those who question whether Barrès succeeds in applying these ideas to his own life. Miéville asserts that Barrès is always too wrapped in himself to feel sympathy for the distress of others.[22] The ideas seem to be greater than the man, according to Miéville.

CHAPTER 9

French Strength and Unity

BARRÈS' call for a strong France is another aspect of his search for the sources of mystic energy. The previous chapter dealt with his attempts to integrate individuals with a superior form of humanity. Barrès believed in addition that nations can use or misuse their spiritual force. As the war drags to a close he remembers his claim, already apparent in *Au Service de l'Allemagne,* that it was up to France to civilize her coarser neighbors.

I   Les diverses familles spirituelles de la France

All through the war Barrès devoted himself to the not particularly easy or inspiring task of keeping up public morale behind the lines. The initial optimism of the first months of fighting were drained by the Russian defeats and by the slow attrition of trench warfare. By 1917, despite some drawbacks, the German forces appeared to be in a strong position. Although fortunately, the Germans did not learn of it, sheer weariness with over two years of incessant fighting caused certain sections of the French army to mutiny. Barrès found himself obliged to strengthen that national unity which sprang into being in 1914 between people of all political convictions, but which diminished as the sense of urgency which had buoyed it was replaced by the feeling that the crisis still left time for normal political backbiting.

In his publication, Barrès intends to shame the quarrelers at home by showing how the same disparate ideas have been unified within the ranks of the army. This can be adequately done through a careful choice of letters to quote and examples to give. Barrès' final picture seems one-sided but to convince his public of the vitality of nationalism in the army he is willing to imply that the individuals he presents are representative of the whole.

Three of the groups with which Barrès deals are religious and two are political. In these last two there is so much confusion with religion that it is easy to acquiesce with his son's claim in the preface that the work is aligned with the three major preoccupations of Barrès' later life — genius, heroism and religious mysticism.[1] Barrès contends that the sufferings of war have refined the human spirit, while the sufferings of France have refined nationalist sentiment.

He deals first with the Catholics, particularly with the priests, whether attached to the army as priests or simply as ordinary soldiers. There can be no doubt that on the whole, Catholic priests showed a remarkable bravery in bringing comfort and assistance to the wounded at the front. Robert Graves recounts the case of colonel who obtains the services of a man of the cloth his soldiers can admire by claiming a 100 percent rate of conversion to Catholicism among the men under his command.[2] Whatever the reason for the priests' courage, it infuses the soldiers with the same will to bravery. From here, Barrès' prose rises to a panegyric of the notion that by their sacrifice and suffering the simple soldiers are redeeming the sins of others. The imagery is beautiful, as is the image of the cross as the symbol of sacrifice redeeming the whole of France. The poetry however, belongs solely to Barrès' personal interpretation. He is not describing others as they are, but rather inciting them to be as he likes to imagine them. The fervor he describes is his own, but he hopes that others will pick it up through emulation. Barrès presents a lie in the hope that the lie can become truth.

Catholic doctrine, Catholic saints, Catholic ceremony: all these are familiar to Barrès. He is not so familiar with Protestantism, however, and his views are colored by the suspicion that Protestantism is not in harmony with the French spirit. It is one of his readers who reminds him that in the Cévennes, as in many areas of Southern France, Huguenots had been rooted in French culture for years. Since Barrès himself regards Protestants from the abstract point of view of the outsider, he tends to consider them as rather cold, calculating beings, moved more by abstract moral precepts than by enthusiasm. For years, Barrès has scorned rationalism and relied on his instincts when making his choices. Now he is at a loss to explain how the Protestants can make the same choices through a process of reason rather than by instinct. His attempts to emulate Protestant feats of biblical commentary are laughable. He explains, for example, that to love one's neighbor as oneself means that you should love your neighbor when he is in trouble, but not when he makes trouble.[3] He is more subtle in his claim that the Germans are narrow and sectarian in their affirmation that God is on their side. One should not say that God is on this or that particular side, but that He is on the side of universal justice. Of course, everyone knows that the French are on the side of universal justice as well. God is not on their side but they are on God's side. The French can raise themselves to the level of the divine, but the Germans can only lower the divine to the level of humanity. The view fits in well with Barrès' often stated view of French and German civilizations. He claims that the war will eventually result in an overall increase in the level of world civilization. One can only regret, with Somerset Maugham, that the Almighty should so often choose such wasteful methods of carrying out His master plan.

If Barrès is a little ill at ease with Protestants, he is even further removed from sympathetic understanding of the Jews, despite his heroic efforts to close the gap. It comes as a surprise to see his condescending attitude towards Theodore Herzl[4] when one might expect him to be interested in the creation of Jewish nationalism. Jewish nationalism possesses all the qualities which attract Barrès — mysticism, enthusiasm, heroism, sentimentality — yet he shrugs his shoulders and turns aside because by nationalism he generally means French nationalism. His approval of Jews is proportional to the extent to which they sacrifice themselves for the French cause. He attempts to claim that in the case of Jewish families domiciled for several generations in France their Judaism is virtually obliterated. He never understands that it is possible for two cultures to co-exist in peace without one surpassing the other. The notion that one can be sincerely French and at the same time sincerely Jewish is foreign to his view of French civilization as a superior culture, an ideal to which all other cultures should aspire.

He takes a similar attitude towards Socialism, making it plain that in his view, Socialists are good Frenchmen to the extent that they are nationalists. It is true of course, that most Socialists put aside their dreams of international fraternity with the onset of the war. Barrès goes further, claiming that the ideals of Socialism have been betrayed by the German brethren and that Germany needs to be destroyed first before the struggle for the ideals of peace and fraternity can be resumed.

Few Socialists were naive enough to be taken in by Barrès' portrayal of France as the champion of Socialism. As the war dragged on, the unions grew powerful and began to agitate for the rights of French workers whom they believed were being exploited by capitalists among the French and their allies. The sense of alienation grew until by 1918, the majority which had supported the "sacred" union when France entered the war had dwindled to a minority. With the war's end Socialists were anxious to resume the class struggle, quite unaffected by Barrès' hope that the fighting might have knocked some nationalist sense into their heads.

Filled as it is with extracts from patriotic letters from the front sent by Frenchmen who were generally killed in heroic action shortly afterwards, the book is a momentarily successful piece of propaganda and powerful incentive to continue the fight. One is a little disappointed, however, that Barrès does not do more to explain the growth of heroism and self-sacrifice. He notes the presence of these ideals with satisfaction, but his explanations of how they come into being and his predictions of how they will affect the personality are too glib and rationalized. The spark of interest animating his studies of Pascal or Joan of Arc is missing here. It cannot return until after the war when he can again devote himself to what he wants to do, as well as what he thinks he ought to do.

II   Le Génie du Rhin

It is under this title that Barrès publishes the lectures he was invited to present at the University of Strasbourg. The main thrust of his argument here tends to support the maintenance of separate Rhineland states, independent from centralized Prussian domination. To disguise this pragmatic modern policy of divide and rule, Barrès delves into history in an attempt to prove that every praiseworthy element in the Rhineland states is a legacy from France and that every Prussian influence has tended, despite occasional appearances to the contrary, to be harmful and destructive. As a result, Barrès claims, it is up to the French to follow a policy which will enable their neighbors to liberate themselves through raising their level of culture. The theme of spiritual discipline which plays such a large part in Barrès' life and works appears once more in these pages. The French nation is urged to discipline itself the better to pass its lessons on to its protégés.

Barrès denies the accusation of attempting to annex, assimilate or conspire against the Rhineland states. On the other hand, he claims that the French have the right to try and extend their influence over the region because the war has left France sufficiently strong to be expansionist. His main argument is a cultural and a racial one. The Rhineland peoples belong to the Latin races and possess the same type of temperament as the French. As a result, cooperation and understanding between the two should be facilitated. His contentions are simply based on the fact that when Napoleon overran the area after the French Revolution, certain segments of the population cooperated with the designated representatives of French authority. Using this sort of argument, it should be equally possible to prove that Alsace-Lorraine is really German at heart.

Barrès fails to make an explicit distinction between the terms "German" and "Prussian," although he does appear to use them differently. "Prussian" is a term of opprobrium. Barrès believes that the strong admixture of slavic elements in the Prussian temperament renders them untrustworthy and irremediably hostile to French culture. He also characterizes as "Prussian" the expansionist energies combined with the tendency to centralize, and the bureaucracy, sometimes cumbersome and sometimes efficient, accompanying it. "German" is a more general term and can apply to any of the states of the old Holy Roman Empire. At times however, Barrès' dislike of things Prussian is retained when he considers things German. His conclusion in this first lecture is that the Germans have few native qualities to boast of and that their culture is based on French borrowings. He even affirms that German mysticism, much vaunted by French Romantic writers, has been originally derived from France through Belgium and Holland.

With the German reputation for mysticism disposed of, Barrès is able to reach his conclusion that the difference between Frenchman and German is that the latter is materialistic and barbarian, lacking the culture and the sensitivity that distinguishes the former. Unfortunately, Barrès' aggressive nationalism has led him to overstate his case. Despite his claims to culture, Barrès does not read widely[5] and is unfamiliar with the work of Schiller, Lessing or Heine. His attitude towards Goethe is revealing. He dwells a great deal on Goethe's studies in Strasbourg and Goethe's desire to speak French well, but neglects to describe how Goethe was rebuffed by the local representatives of French culture, and how this rejection served as a springboard for the development of his German heritage. Under the guise of bringing culture to ignorant German natives, Barrès is ultimately laying claim to control of German territory. The lectures are justifications, to himself and to others, of France's moral right to interfere in German affairs.

Barrès' next lecture deals with legends and ruins, representing what he calls the sensibility, or spirit of the region. He makes a telling point when he claims that a people is what their dreams are made of. With this in mind, Barrès examines German legends and finds that the principal actors are generally the magician, the damned, and the victim, all of whom move in a setting of savagery, hostility and fearful mystery. When the same legends arrive in the Rhineland, they are humanized by Latin and Celtic influences. The magical characters become helpful rather than malevolent. Man is able to defend himself against sorcery by affirming his sense of justice and honor. The French attitude implies a sense of moderation and self-control, while the German attitude implies self-immolation to superior forces. Barrès sees the same attitudes at work in the interpretation of the lives of historical figures. The Germans glorify harsh despots, while the Rhineland follows the French fashion of adulating characters who have exercised a civilizing influence. Barrès concludes that it is up to representatives of French culture to make every effort to bring the myths of the Rhineland closer to the French outlook.

Having proved to his own satisfaction that the people of the Rhineland are temperamentally akin to their French neighbors, Barrès concerns himself in his last lecture with outlining ways in which this kinship can be exploited for mutual benefit. He conceives of the region as ultimately becoming an autonomous entity, free from France and Germany, but serving first as a buffer zone, then as a link between the two. He speaks of developing the cultural independence of the region, although he naturally assumes that it would lean more towards France than Germany. His last suggestion is indicative of his attitude. Casting round for a symbol on which to build the cultural identity of the people, he can think of no better figure than Joan of Arc. She symbolizes the good and the creative. She seeks to liberate people so that they can realize their full potential. Her memory has remained vivid in the Rhineland. Almost a native of Lorraine, she is worthy to inspire the people of

Alsace-Lorraine to be in the forefront of the task of civilizing their neighbors. Their historical role has been to act as a first line of defense, adapting German attitudes to become like superior French ones, but now it is time to take the offensive. Barrès does not know exactly how his projects will be realized, but as in *Au Service de l'Allemagne,* he appears to have an unshakeable confidence in the capacity of civilization to absorb and transform the elements of barbarity which assail it.

III   Pour la haute intelligence française

Barrès did not have the time to make the alterations to this material he might have wished. He had done no more than outline his general intentions when death overtook him. We know in some detail, however, what he would have written because many of his notes are adaptations of the articles he had already written concerning the development of scientific research.

The main thrust of his purpose is made clear when he speaks of his proposed work as another aspect of his campaign in favor of the restoration of French churches. It is not so much science for itself that interests Barrès, but science as a representation of the French spirit and French traditions. As often happens, the affirmation of French superiority is uttered as a defiance of Germany and German methods. It is often difficult in Barrès to disentangle the two themes, fear of Germany and pride in France.

It is fear of Germany which comes through first, mingled with a reluctant respect for German methods of work and organization. Barrès is all too aware that France, like Britain and America, is embarking upon the decade of the "gay twenties," but he hopes that the sybaritic pleasures in which his countrymen indulge do not dull their moral values or capacity for sacrifice to higher ideals. Barrès insists that if France is to remain viable as a political and industrial force, she must emulate Germany in all aspects of her organization. He creates some complications for himself however, when he attempts to link scientific superiority with moral superiority. It is difficult to grasp how the wartime invention of a superior French poison gas demonstrates moral richness.[6] On the whole, however, despite some contradictions, it is the notion of human unity in scientific development which lies behind all of his thought.

There is little doubt that Barrès sincerely believes that of all modern nations, France is most capable of carrying the torch of civilization. The development of purely national interests does not preclude the development of a more general internationalism. On the contrary, a strong state will be a strong leader in the effort towards civilized progress. Barrès envisages France as the director of an international community.[7] The main question is one of moral and intellectual superiority from which political superiority will naturally flow, provided that no obstacles are put in the path of economic development. Unfortunately, lack of proper scientific and technological development does constitute a major obstacle, and it is this obstacle Barrès attempts to remove.

There is something a little out of place in Barrès' confidence in science as expressed in these pages. He had begun his writing career at a time when Brunetière had proclaimed the "bankruptcy" of science; and although Barrès himself had never launched a thoroughgoing attack on science, he had also largely ignored it. Science does not fit into his world. He is not alone in this attitude; for the majority of his contemporaries, arts and letters, law and politics are immeasurably more important. Now Barrès chooses to present science with the confidence one feels in displaying a universal panacea. The views he expresses are those of Zola twenty years before, that science and the scientific method will solve man's social problems. Aware since his youth of workers' movements, Barrès seeks to include the workers in his grand coalition of industry, laboratories and teaching institutions. They will no longer have to fight, he thinks, to obtain a (still inadequate) portion of the national production. Science can increase production so that with no extra effort, there will be more than enough for everybody. In this respect, France can give example to the world.

Times have now changed and we are in a period where science is regarded as a destroyer of resources, rather than a creator of plenty. Perhaps the pendulum will swing again and we will come closer to Barrès' confident predictions. In any event, there is an attractive enthusiasm in this man, almost sixty years old, writing confidently of the benefits of science.

When Barrès begins his campaign in favor of scientific development, he works closely with eminent scientists of his acquaintance and presents the ideas they would like to see adopted.Many of his suggestions have been put into practice in modern society, particularly in America. The awarding of scholarships to promising stu-

dents, through national bodies and through industry, is a fulfillment of Barrès' ideas, as is the awarding of assistantships to gradu-
ate students to enable them to gain practical experience while paying their way through their respective programs. Salaries are open-
ended and differ from one institution to another, while a healthy
spirit of competition has replaced the old seniority system. Other of
his ideas have won a certain popularity. He advocates, for example,
using the combined resources of a particular region to set up spe-
cialized institutes. This notion corresponds naturally to his desire
for decentralized education and a large measure of local autonomy.
It is also easier, over a small area, to set up checks against duplica-
tion of work which would otherwise waste all too scarce resources
France has on hand.

For publicity purposes, Barrès claims that a strong scientific
corps should be created first, before bothering about what impetus
it should be given. In the *Cahiers,* however, Barrès does show himself deeply concerned with the ends to which science might be put.[8]
Science without humanism, he claims, will become an evil power
bent on destruction. In this respect he feels that the French are
superior to the Germans because only France, through a combination of science and the religious spirit will be capable of checking
the inhumanity in German progress. Man is debased by being
purely materialistic. Science must therefore be infused with charity
and the humanistic spirit, the most eminent guardian of which is
the church.

CHAPTER 10

The Final Years

MYSTICISM and French cultural expansion are inextricably joined in the last two works to be published in Barrès' lifetime. They are works of diverse character, one being a purely fictional account which wells from his imagination, the second being an account of Barrès trip through the Middle East just before the onset of the First World War.

I Une enquête aux pays du Levant

Despite complications caused by postponement of the publication of his journal the possibility of French cultural and economic expansion and his increasing interest in mysticism cause Barrès to dust off his old notes. His political comments belong to the postwar period when France, along with the other victorious powers is scrambling to take over the bits and pieces of the dismantled Ottoman empire and extend her political and economic influence in the Middle East. The change is most marked in Barrès' attitude towards the minority groups in the area. At the outset of his journey the French ambassador in Constantinople has tried to persuade him that France's best interest lies in maintaining the Ottoman empire, keeping Turkey herself strong, then doing business with the Turks.[1] After the war the power of Turkey is so broken that nothing can restore it. France's only hope is to appear anti-Turkish and support the formerly oppressed minorities as they struggle to define their nationhood.

It is in the land of one of these minority groups, Lebanon, that Barrès encounters the ruined temple of Afaka where maenads once worked themselves into orgiastic frenzies. Barrès is attracted, not by the purely physical aspects of the revelry, but by the underlying religious principles. The orgy is simply the distorted development

142

of an originally noble impulse, a degraded mechanical means of achieving a state of grace. In his thirst for knowledge man has always run the risk that the unknown is a powerful force which will not allow itself to be dominated. The maenads are individuals who have been destroyed by the forces they unwittingly let loose. There is some discrepancy between what Barrès hopes and what he actually encounters. It is his hope that since at the origin of all mystic movements there is a central core of purity, the dross will eventually be purged away and spiritual motives will imbue all of the participants' aspirations. He is forced to recognize, however, that if not mastered, the mystic impulse seems to act as a destructive force reducing the would-be adepts to expressing themselves in terms of animalistic passions. Faced with the question whether it is worth the risk to throw oneself into the mystic adventure, Barrès unhesitatingly adopts the affirmative view. He has no esteem for the timid man who prudently refrains from testing himself against the unknown thereby denying his innate drive for knowledge, but praises the man who is driven to enlarge his horizons through heroic effort.

His reflection on the manifestations of long dead fertility cults leads quickly into the problem how much sensuality is present in contemporary religious cults. He knows that Catholicism easily absorbs old pagan beliefs and wonders to what extent it has succeeded in purifying them and directing the energies they release toward constructive ends. An answer of sorts is afforded by a young Maronite girl, Hendiye. A mistake is made when she is put in charge of others before she learns self-discipline. Characters such as she, imbued with patent spiritual force, have the capacity to attract around them those whose designs are more base. All is well if these disciples are kept in check by firm discipline and constant vigilance. Hendiye, however, is incapable of tearing herself away from meditation in order to devote herself to practical matters of government. Unrestrained, the grosser nature of her companions perverts the spiritual energies which they contact and makes them revert to the carnal excesses of the past. Hendiye expiates her misrule by living as a simple nun in an obscure convent until her death some twenty years later. Although he does not openly say so, Barrès' conclusion seems to be that even for the church, the process of purification is a long and arduous one with constant backsliding. Without the church however, chaos prevails. Hasan Sabah, leader of the assassins, is fascinating for his energy, fanaticism and determination. He is a man of vision, but all his power is turned to destructive ends.

In the town of Konya, Barrès encounters a quite different type of mysticism practiced by a group of dervishes who seek to bring on spiritual enlightenment through the use of music and the dance, rather than the drugs that Hasan Sabah employs. The fundamental difference is that dancing dervishes do not attempt to found any kind of militant order to spread their methods and beliefs among other people. They are quite content to seek individual spiritual salvation. This very individualism and flexibility appears to be rather baffling for Barrès who is more at ease with fixed rules of conduct and experiences which will apply to everybody. He is dismayed to hear that a novice cannot know at the outset what road he will travel nor how long it will take him to become an adept; and he tends to ascribe this uncertainty to a shortcoming in the doctrine itself. If a person does not experience the same sensations as everyone else in the group, Barrès tends to accuse him of dangerous individualism threatening to discipline and order. There are, however, several other features of the sect that Barrès thinks coincide with his own views. The dervishes appear to accept the uselessness of knowledge as opposed to inner illumination. One of the founders is an ignorant peasant but ennobled by divine grace. One cannot but think that in this respect he is an Eastern counterpart of Joan of Arc. Despite this reference to divine grace, however, dervishes believe with Barrès that mystic fulfillment is not vouchsafed out of nothing but has to be worked for to be achieved. This struggle for achievement forms a safeguard against excess. It is the self-discipline which prevents the adept from falling into chaos.

According to what Barrès learns of the life and thought of the founders, the dance certainly seems to be effective in leading to states which he envies, but which he is afraid to emulate himself. The goal to be achieved is absorption in God — the loss of all sense of self in union with something greater. Barrès is quite familiar with this aim, practiced by the Quietists of the eighteenth century and ridiculed by Zola.[2] On a more pedestrian level it is the state Barrès himself attempts to achieve through total identification with his country. As a writer he feels he has sometimes achieved contact with perfection after the creation of a particularly satisfactory piece of prose. Like the dance, creative writing can be regarded as a mechanical means of setting in motion the movement towards spiritual harmony.

The quality common to any state of mystic transport is its transitoriness. Tension can be maintained only for a limited time, after which the adept sinks back into everyday reality with only the memory of his ecstasy to comfort him. Between periods of higher union he experiences a cool indifference to the enjoyment of earthly pleasures, seeking only pure companionship enabling him to live through periods of relaxation when he is not caught up in mystic transport. The nineteenth century decadent's suspicion of sexuality, combined with Middle Eastern contempt for woman as mere chattel causes Barrès to reject physical love as too dangerous a challenge to the purity and serenity which represent the true divinity.

For all his enthusiasm, Barrès' attraction for the Konya mystics seems somewhat hollow. Although he can study texts which describe the rapture of others, and even watch the dervishes as they dance themselves into a trance for him, he cannot acquire the same experiences for himself. He is always asking how mystic enlightenment is achieved, but is never willing to undertake the process of initiation himself, to find out at first hand exactly what goes on. He is in too much of a hurry, and through wanting to understand everything at once, understands nothing.

It is quite evident that the dervishes find contentment through the dance, but because he cannot understand why, Barrès expresses a slight contempt for the peace of mind he previously praises. More true to the warrior tradition of Loyola, he prefers a doctrine which attempts to force contentment on others, as well as brings contentment to oneself. As a writer, Barrès likes to think of himself as an artistic Loyola, leading others as well as himself to an appreciation of their own full potentialities. All these factors combine to produce in Barrès a dissatisfaction with whatever form of mysticism he finds in the East. Some adepts err on the side of violence, misdirecting the energies of mysticism into orgiastic or murderous ceremonies. Other mystics fall into the sin of omission, attracting around them forces which they cannot control, although they remain uncontaminated while those around them are destroyed. Others fall into complacency and fail to use their enlightenment for the benefit of others. It follows that the East, though still possessing tremendous potential energy, is incapable of guiding this energy to good purpose.

At this point the theme of mysticism is linked with the theme of colonialism. It is up to the West to lend a guiding hand, provide the discipline the East cannot develop for itself. The Western representative most fitted to undertake this task is the Catholic church, through the missions which it already has set up throughout the area. Barrès never for a moment thinks that the influence of the church might be anything other than beneficial. Ignoring the historical evidence that Catholicism has had its share of schismatics, forgetting that he himself has dealt with the history of such a splinter group in *La Colline inspirée,* he credits Catholic missionaries with the power to guide the people as well as the will to submit to higher authority.

Perhaps without realizing it, Barrès had modified the opinions he outlines earlier. Once he favored the authority of Rome, claiming that it represents a superior civilizing influence in local areas of France. Now Barrès claims that the authority of Rome is at its most effective only where it reflects French culture and civilization. He faces a problem here which he has to deal with again in his reports to parliament urging the reestablishment of teaching orders in France. The orders of which he speaks are international, bound by vows of obedience to Rome and owing no particular allegiance to France.[3] Traditionally, however, French brothers have always played a prominent role in the activities of orders in the Middle East. More broadly, Barrès claims that since France is the most advanced Latin civilization, the spread of Catholicism cannot help but favor French expansion. All the same, Barrès is a realist underneath the rhetoric and knows that the best way to insure that the orders serve French interests is to fill them with Frenchmen. The orders themselves will not cease to exist. Rather than see them taken over by Italians and Spaniards — or even worse, Germans or Anglo-Saxons — Barrès prefers promoting the training of French brethren to fill the gaps.

The key to understanding Barrès' attitude is his nationalism and the fact that after the war he knows he is addressing a parliament in which nationalism is the dominant factor. In such a situation, it is easy to believe what is best for France is best for everyone. He defends French interest, not for the sake of France alone, but for the sake of humanity. There is singleness of identification between the altruism of the church and the altruism of France. It follows that France seeks to dominate the orders not just to repulse for-

eigners and protect French interests, but because this is the best way
to maintain the purity of the church's intentions against the schismatics from within who seek to corrupt it. By token of the same
identification, France becomes not just a secular nation, but a
defender of the faith and flower of the church, carrying the banner
of civilization high for others to follow. Something of the eternity
of the church is conferred on France. Something of French secular
interests is transferred to the church.

Thanks to the identification of nationalism and Catholicism,
everything becomes clear-cut and simple. The heroes and villains
are easy to identify. Judgment can be made from a single point of
view which is indubitably the correct one. The two criteria that
Barrès uses are religion and race. His hatred for Islam is expressed
trenchantly in terms which brook no contradiction. It matters little
to him that the once fertile Mesopotamian plains had been barren
long before the birth of the Prophet. He blames Islam for denuding
the land of vegetation and casting the people into misery. He
recounts the misfortunes of a French businessman in Turkey in
order to prove that the Turks are utterly xenophobic and refuse to
apply their own laws to foreigners when it is to the latter's advantage. The Turkish attitude is the somewhat understandable one of a
majority uneasy in the presence of large foreign minorities. In his
youth Barrès had adopted a similar attitude to the Jewish minority
in France, suggesting that measures be taken to curb the rights of
this minority, although his violent suggestion had been mainly ver-
bal, not approaching the actual violence the Turks had attained
during the 1896 massacres of the Armenians.

Barrès is opposed to Turkey because the Turkish cultural tradition is quite alien to him. Culturally, as well as politically, he is
motivated to favor the aspirations of those minorities whom the
Turks oppress, provided that they are Christian. The Jewish
minorities are only twice mentioned in his account. In the first in-
stance, he speaks favorably of two Alsatian brothers who renounce
Judaism to carry out spectacularly successful work as Christian
missionaries. In the second, he repeats the long discredited allega-
tion of ritual Jewish blood murders, dwelling on the combination
of blood, violence and death in a throwback to the themes of *Du
Sang, de la Volupté et de la Mort*. The Christian minorities on the
other hand he considers brothers whom France has a duty to lead to
nationhood. Established Turkish nationalism is decried, but the

latent nationalism of the minorities is fostered. Faced with two or more conflicting nationalisms, Barrès unhesitatingly chooses the culture with which he can identify most closely in the belief that this will prove to be the culture most friendly and advantageous to his own country.

After religion, race and culture are the second criterion for judging heroes and villains. Barrès' prejudices favor his own Aryan race. The initial pages are full of confused impressions, questions of whether the Turkish peasant is Aryan and the Turkish aristocrat, Mongol; whether the Islamic religion overcomes the virtues of the Aryan race; whether the strong Georgian and Circassian admixture in Constantinople constitutes a race apart. His broad purpose is to show that any non-aryan culture represents a foreign overlay at odds with the general tradition of the region. He pins his hopes mainly on the Hittite civilization, which ruled in the area from 1800 to 1200 B.C., and which contemporary investigations are beginning to show probably belonged to an aryan offshoot.[4] He believes that if it can be shown that the whole cultural underpinning of the region is Aryan, then he is justified in encouraging minorities to return to a culture whose most fruitful developments France already displays in her own cultural traditions. It will be natural for these interrelated peoples to work in harmony, while the dangers of "uprootedness" will be correspondingly diminished. Barrès is fully alert to the dangers of destroying cultural roots by way of an overdose of French civilization. To some extent this is another reason for working with the Christian minorities who are closer to Europe than the representatives of Islam.

The thorny question nonetheless remains how these minorities are to be prodded into self-development without alienating them from their traditions. Will the elite group with which the teaching orders inevitably deal be willing to enter into a working alliance with the West? Barrès shudders at the thought of uprooted, unoccupied, discontented young people throwing themselves into a ferment of political, social and religious revolution. He calls upon them to cast off the Turkish yoke, but he does not intend them to become undisciplined advocates of social chaos.

The question of French interest is uppermost in his thoughts. Is it possible for East and West to harmonize in these young students? When Barrès speaks of the West he specifically means France.[5] To avoid the danger of pupils turning against their teachers, Barrès suggests that stress be laid on the links between two contiguous aryan civilizations, and that the two cultures, springing from the same stock, be brought together as close as possible. He believes the French culture can be the yeast to ensure the rise of an indigenous culture inextricably mingled with it. Colonialism is primarily cultural. If two civilizations feel themselves to be close, then trade agreements and other commercial paraphernalia readily follow.

At this time Islam is vigorously proselytizing to indigenous populations of the Middle East and Africa. Wherever it takes hold there arises a forceful nationalism determinedly opposed to the European colonial powers. Barrès aim in supporting the teaching orders is to allow them to get in first, inoculate the people against the pan-Islam virus, predispose them to cooperation with France. France's role is the one it has claimed to play since the revolution, a beacon of enlightenment guiding all peoples to the highest possible degree of civilization.

It is with this role in mind that Barrès attacks Germany for consistently appealing to the dark, destructive side of human nature. Countless examples appear to confirm his prejudices. The attraction Schopenhauer felt for Oriental philosophy had strengthened. The Germans had developed a cult of death and nothingness, a cult that was also latent in the religions of the Middle East but which needed to be vigorously opposed by the Christian forces of life and light. Spengler, prophet of doom and destruction, cannot but arouse Barrès' wrath, as does Freud, discoverer of a murky unconscious which abases mankind. Germany is not capable of civilizing the Orient. Only France is sufficiently strong for this task, and Barrès expresses again his old hope that France will filter out whatever is dangerous in Eastern civilization and produce a synthesis of the best in East and West which will benefit everyone. Then France can justly claim its predestined position as spiritual leader of the civilized world. Barrès' obvious altruism and greatness of purpose shine through with a vitality that does credit to a man who, seeing every day the baseness of human nature in parliament can yet believe in man's latent nobility.

II   Un Jardin sur l'Oronte

It is something of a surprise that this novel should be written at such a late stage in Barrès' career. Readers and critics alike are certainly taken aback by the ardent sensuality of its orientalism, and not a few criticize him for publishing a type of work which they are unaccustomed to seeing under his name. Barrès is rather hurt by their attacks, since he persists in the conviction that he remains true to his own nature, and that to accuse him of some kind of self-betrayal is to try and enclose his personality in too rigid a box of Catholic nationalism.[6] In composing his novel, Barrès casts his mind back to the highly charged exoticism which has been among his main preoccupations twenty years before. As the basis of his composition he uses a short account which he had written at that earlier time, *La Musulmane courageuse*.[7] It is unfair, however, to regard this latter story as a first draft of *Un Jardin sur l'Oronte*. It serves rather as a springboard from which Barrès launches himself into his new novel. All that remains of the original in the later work is a bare skeleton of events, a scanty outline of the two main characters and a few artistically appealing passages which Barrès transposes from one work to the other, although not without introducing some modifications.

The hero of *La Musulmane courageuse* is Mazdali, a half-Norman, half-Arab *métis*. Despite his exotic background, he is to all intents and purposes a turn-of-the-century French decadent who, particularly with regard to women, believes that he has experienced all possible sensations and that he can henceforth look forward only to repetition of unchanging human sentiments. Mixed in with this feeling of surfeit is the desire to return to the place of his birth, to which the many generations which precede him have given a special, indefinable atmosphere arousing in Mazdali a feeling of satisfaction and contentment.

When he finally makes the acquaintance of the anonymous *musulmane,* the entire focus of his life shifts towards her. All the values of his birthplace are transferred to the woman. As for her, Barrès' epithet "courageous" seems strange when applied to her. She is not in a situation where courage can normally make its presence felt. She is a slave, subject to the caprice of her master and accustomed all her life to being regarded as an inferior. It is true that beneath the surface, there is a hint of hidden depths which may conceal a certain dangerous energy. She is intelligent, but she has been able to use her qualities to gain only a semblance of freedom. It is impossible to imagine what she is capable of if all her capacities are put into action; circumstances deny her the opportunity.

Her city is besieged by the Christians, her lord the Emir is killed, the defenders finally capitulate and the women pass, along with the rest of the booty, into the hands of the conquerors. After a brief period of service as an interpreter, Mazdali is packed off home to Cordoba. Unable to bear separation from his beloved, he returns in disguise to find that she is the favorite of the Christian leader. Her refusal to die with him justifies the use of the term "courageous" to describe her. Her major strengths are acceptance of whatever events impose themselves, and the capacity for compliance with which she molds herself to these events. She accepts life in all its aspects, and in this respect constitutes a salutary lesson for the decadent whose thoughts are dominated by the death wish, and who oscillates between contemplation and frenetic action (undertaken in a usually inconclusive effort to stave off boredom). The account ends with a tableau of the three of them: Mazdali, the Christian leader, and his mistress together in the garden. The trio forms a dynamic but unbalanced group perpetually forging for itself the bitter joys to be tasted only when hovering on the brink of disaster. In a sense, the moral is pessimistic because it highlights the impossibility for Mazdali of finding satisfaction and happiness. In another sense however, the moral is more optimistic, for through the woman slave, Barrès affirms the value of life, no matter what shape it takes.

Un Jardin sur l'Oronte is a more mature work than *La Musulmane courageuse* and contains deeper implications. Still under the influence of his long trip through the Middle East, Barrès transfers the location of his story from Arab Spain to Syria, under the crusaders. Mazdali "becomes" Guillaume, a full-blooded Frankish knight drawn by the crusades to seek his fortune. Traces of Mazdali's origins are present in the supposed *métis* author of the text on which Barrès bases his account of the love between Guillaume and Oriante, the name given to the previously anonymous woman. Guillaume is a little like Mazdali, not because he is so sated, but in so far as he is looking for some kind of supreme ideal whose description defies the imagination. Because of past influences in his life, notably his mother's comments, this ideal takes the form of a woman to love.

From the outset, Barrès links Guillaume's aspirations with the Tristan and Isolde legend. The reader is warned that the story revolves around the twin themes of love and despair. Barrès appears to contradict, however, the emphasis on fatalism which runs through the legend, implying that acquiescence to fate is only for the weak. It is insofar as Guillaume reflects certain tendencies of the decadent type that Barrès discreetly implies criticism of his attitudes. Guillaume, when he has attained a supreme moment of happiness, tends to long for death to engulf him, precisely because he has reached a summit from which he can only descend. Happiness is perceived not as long-lasting, but as a moment of perfection rising above an eternity of mediocrity. Mazdali experiences the same curious death wish which seems peculiarly Romantic and can be traced back to Rousseau's Saint-Preux.[8] Barrès characterizes this yearning as an absurdity, worthy only of a man insufficiently energetic to impose a direction on his own life.

To Guillaume Barrès contrasts Oriante. Although a slave, she puts into effect all the latent energy that her predecessor appears to possess, but with greater success. Because she is aware of her own nature and desires she is able to control herself and also to exercise control over others who lack this awareness. In both versions, the somewhat remarkable act of the Arab prince to allow his foreign guest to see his favorite, is attributed by Barrès to surreptitious maneuverings on her part. In the first case however, it is because she has already conceived an attraction for Mazdali, while in the second version she wishes only to introduce a new distraction into the harem. Even when she sends Isabelle to Guillaume to act as a go-between there is some doubt that she does so out of affection. Her main purpose seems to be to use herself as a lure to attach Guillaume more firmly to the city and its well-being, for she is aware that Qalaat is threatened by many enemies and sees in Guillaume a potential defender more capable than the ineffectual Emir.

Oriante reveals herself an energetic personality both willing and able to twist the course of events to her own advantage. When the Emir is killed during an imprudent sally outside the city walls there is some suspicion that the arrow which killed him was fired from within his own ranks. Is this an expression of the general discontent against his harsh rationing policies and his confiscation of the peasants' corn to feed his soldiers? Or was there a plot calculated by Oriante to rid herself of him? Certainly, she refuses to accept the principles of social conduct which lead to the unfulfilled yearnings and the doomed love of Tristan and Isolde. Her naive question as to why Tristan does not do away with Mark is a direct invitation to Guillaume to assassinate the Emir, which he cannot take up because he is steeped in the traditions of his own society. When Oriante sees that the siege is lost, she takes the initiative and contacts the Christian leader herself.

In this respect she distinguishes herself quite clearly from her predecessor (who waited for events to engulf her). In the first story it is three days before the Christian leader thinks of halting the looting and carnage. In the later version, it is only a matter of hours, because Oriante has offered herself and the riches of the city as recompense for clemency. Oriante as a slave has been obliged to perfect the art of dissimulation. All the other women of the harem follow her example to such good effect that Guillaume, when he returns from Damascus where he had been tricked into fleeing after the city's collapse, can hardly believe that the group of perfectly adapted Christian women he encounters had once been the delight of the Emir's harem, and strict devotees of Islam.

Guillaume never succeeds in assimilating fully the lessons to be learned from a sense of his own impotence. When he languishes in Damascus, he refuses to wait patiently until the time is ripe for the local Emir to send him to Qalaat as his ambassador, a position in which he would have enjoyed considerable advantages and scope of action. Instead, he flees secretly to Qalaat where he arrives miserable and penniless and in no position to undertake any decisive action at all. When finally, through the initiative of Oriante, he is accepted as a Frankish comrade into the palace of the Christian leader, he throws away all the advantages of dissimulation in an uncontrolled outburst of temper and gets himself killed for his trouble by the other outraged knights.

Guillaume is an individual who does not really know himself, or what he wants. He has left France in pursuit of an undefined vision of happiness. Barrès goes so far as to hint that Guillaume's happiness depends to some extent on the non-fulfillment of his ambitions. Happiness is not a total union which (if it occurs at all) is fleeting and casts a shadow over future pleasures, but rather the promise of total union. Guillaume's fascination with Oriante persists because even when he has overcome the physical barrier between them and is in her arms, he still cannot reach her.

Although Guillaume is not fully conscious of this contradiction in his aspirations — if he had become conscious of it, it would have disappeared — it does block his will to action. Because he is not fully aware of what he really wants, his actions are often ineffectual and cause him suffering. His first indecisive act is to remain in the fortress while it is beleaguered by his fellow Christians. If it is for desire of Oriante that he stays, there are much more effective ways to obtain her. He can have joined the attackers and claimed her as his share of the booty. To do this would have been against his honor — as it would have been against his honor to assassinate the Emir. For similar reasons, he prefers to conduct a defensive siege rather than take aggressive steps against his comrades-in-religion. He is not single-minded in his actions and does not want Oriante exclusive of all else. If Guillaume is "poisoned" by Orientalism, it is because he does not truly possess himself. He allows himself to become the plaything of outside influences, either Oriante, or conventional notions of honor; the contradiction between the two finally destroys him.

Oriante on the other hand, is quite clear about what she wants. She is primarily attracted to riches and power. She first turns her attentions to Guillaume because he seems much more efficient and energetic than the Emir, who has grown soft in the enjoyment of the luxuries of his palace. Oriante aspires to control others. She knows that she cannot oppose events, but through her clearsightedness, can manipulate them. She becomes increasingly irritated with Guillaume when he fails to recognize her ambition and turns away from him in search of another vehicle for her aspirations. She is ready to admit without any attempt at prevarication that she seeks power, and the riches which are generally the symbol of power. To this end she chooses companions who can further her ambitions. She wishes to reign as queen of Qalaat. Even further, she wishes to impose her personal stamp on the city through an act of creation. When Guillaume returns from Damascus he discovers her directing the transformation of Qalaat into a new, Christianized town. Both she and the bishop work together using the methods that Barrès suggests elsewhere of building on the past, creating a tradition, rooting the children of mixed marriages to the region, forming a new entity with its foundations firmly anchored in the old. Oriante understands herself well enough to recognize that this is her major ambition, the major reason for her existence.

Love is something which is interesting and desirable, but ancillary to her main purpose. Because power is the center of her existence, love does not mean the same thing for her as it does for Guillaume. For him, love is total union, the merging of two identities, utter self-sacrifice on the part of the lovers to attain the ideal of perfection. Oriante on the other hand, represents a more modern notion of love as cooperation and collaboration. Like the heroine of the first version, she accepts life and all the conditions it imposes. She goes much further than passive acceptance however, trying to create out of life something which is meaningful to hers. She believes that she has grounds to criticize Guillaume because instead of helping her actively in her plans, he wavers and shows divided loyalties. When he returns from Damascus she is willing, once she is sure of his loyalty to her, to try and associate him again with her projects; but Guillaume, with his notion of love as total union completely misunderstands her. He dies, symbolically with his eyes closed, so that he can see not her, but rather the vision of perfection which she should be. The novel answers the question posed in *Le Voyage de Sparte* as to why the vitality of French crusaders diminishes. If they are like Guillaume, they are too self-centered. Barrès believes that the pitfalls can be avoided by having the church, not individuals, take over the reconstruction of the Orient.

Although Barrès is far from being a novice when he writes *La Musulmane courageuse,* the later novel gives evidence of greater maturity and skill. The characters are much richer. Their motives, although more complex, are more skillfully presented and explained. The contrast between hero and heroine is made more incisive. The Bergsonian notions of liberty and creativity, barely perceptible in the first version, are crucial to the theme of the second. Minor characters are developed to produce a richer texture and to fill out the ideas in the work. *Un Jardin sur l'Oronte* is not only sensual and passionate, it is the tribute of a sexagenarian to the tenacity, value, and joy of life.

CHAPTER 11

Conclusion

I N 1921, the Surrealists put Barrès "on trial" and found him guilty of subverting the human spirit.[1] Almost immediately following his death Barrès was consigned to that purgatory which seems to be the lot of almost all French writers once their demise removes them from the public.[2] "In 1973," wrote Mauriac, "will there remain a single heart, a single thought to greet his ghost?"[3] Barrès suffers from being identified too closely with a single idea, that of French nationalism. It brought him fame and popularity after the war when a right-wing Chamber ruled, but the swing to the left in the 1924 elections which rehabilitated his old enemies Caillaux and Malvy foreshadowed the discredit of his ideas. To some extent, Barrès himself is to blame. He too often stresses nationalism to the detriment of other aspects of his work. It is true that as early as the *Taches d'encre,* he proclaims the necessity of regaining the occupied territories, but this did not necessarily make him a nationalist.

Barrès' beginnings are far from being political. He is concerned to react against the two major literary schools, Naturalism and Romanticism, and avoid the virtuosity and hyperbole which lead nowhere.[4] He is critical of his predecessors whose speculations seem inevitably to lead to the emptiness of philosophy and the relativity of knowledge. In formulating his reply to these problems Barrès makes himself the acknowledged leader of his generation, yet he seems ill at ease. If compared to Gide, who was engaged in developing his own form of *cult of the self,* Barrès seems to lack self-confidence. He expresses the fear that he will not have the energy to carry on his quest. He seeks to absorb energy from outside sources by linking himself to a greater corporate body.

The quest for sources of energy, more than nationalism, seems to

156

be the constant in Barrès' career. Throughout his life he enlarges the sphere in which he attempts to tap this energy. The *cult of self* quickly reaches its limits. Barrès has to break through and link himself to the outside world. He does this in *Le Jardin de Bérénice,* when Philippe comes into contact with the latent energy of the masses. In actual practice it is the energy of Boulanger which attracts Barrès. With his magnetic personality, Boulanger gives promise of being the means by which the whole French nation can affirm itself forcefully. Boulanger is the first of the figures to whom Barrès is attracted for their vitality.

He seems to have fallen into Socialism almost by accident when assigned to win over the workers in the Nancy constituency. His proposals for economic reform appear at best half-hearted, especially when compared to his ringing calls for political reform.[5] For Barrès, filling the workers' bellies is a preliminary step in the task of bringing them to an awareness of their role as representatives of France and of humanity. From this point on, Barrès appears trapped in a web of his own making where his efforts to get out only entangle him more tightly. It has been pointed out earlier[6] that Barrès' nationalism is a defense against the loneliness of the individual at odds with an absurd and hostile universe. He is always afraid that his main defense, France, may disappear. He is keenly aware that without the intervention — first of England then of America — France would not have survived the war. Even afterward he doubts that France's material power is a match for that of her neighbors. As a result, he feels constrained to defend France first, then humanity.

There are many signs of his efforts to break out of nationalism into a wider field.[7] His *Cahiers* while not altering any judgment of his ideas, present a softer image of the man much more aware of nuances and of the value of human civilization. His most notable effort to expand is in his defense of Catholicism as a booster of spiritual consciousness. His quest for the sources of mystic energy even leads him outside purely Western tradition to the Middle East. He is blocked, however, by his fears of French weakness. He had been able to transcend the comparatively narrow *cult of self* once he was sure of its strength. But he could never be sufficiently sure of French strength to transcend it and develop himself fully as a representative of humanity. As a result, instead of expanding

French consciousness to embrace the whole of humanity Barrès tends to restrict humanity to French values. Fortunately, Barrès is not completely a traditionalist. He is aware that the values of the past can stifle the human spirit if they remain static, without undergoing a process of dynamic evolution. Although this notion is expressed most clearly in his youth, it reappears in his later writings. The Catholic church is blamed for suppressing all possibility of change while in *Le Voyage de Sparte* and *Une enquête aux pays du Levant* he foresees that French civilization will slowly outgrow itself. All of Barrès' efforts to promote syntheses, whether of paganism and Catholicism; science and religion; Socialism and nationalism; France and the Middle East; are efforts to promote growth and change. Miéville claims that there is no unity in Barrès, that "there were in Barrès several different men who were not welded together, and who perhaps, despite his efforts, could not be."[8] This apparent lack of unity is actually Barrès' greatest strength. His continual efforts to surpass himself provide, outside of his publications, his most living example of vitality and creativity.

Notes and References

Chapter One

1. Georges Tronquart, "Barrès et l'Université" in *Actes du Colloque Maurice Barrès organisé par la Faculté des lettres et des sciences de l'Université de Nancy,* (Nancy: Annales de l'Est, 1963), p. 253.
2. *Mes Cahiers,* vol. 7, p. 319.
3. *Ibid.,* vol. 1, p. 21.
4. *Amori et dolori sacrum,* (Paris: Juven, 1903), p. 123.
5. *Ibid.,* p. 129.
6. *Leurs figures,* (Paris: Plon, 1926), p. 326.
7. These letters are published in *Le Départ pour la vie,* (Paris: Plon, 1961).
8. *Le Départ pour la vie,* pp. 45-47.
9. *Ibid.,* p. 111.
10. Jules Renard, *Journal 1887-1910* (Paris: 1960), p. 127.
11. For a brief assessment of Jules Soury's influence on Barrès, see R. Soucy, *Fascism in France; the Case of Maurice Barrès,* (Berkeley: University of California Press, 1972), pp. 140-42.
12. *Le Départ pour la vie,* pp. 197-98.
13. Quoted by Z. Sternhell, *Maurice Barrès et le nationalisme français,* (Paris: Armand Colin, 1972), p. 158.
14. Quoted by Jean Touchard, "Le Nationalisme de Barrès" in *Actes du Colloque Maurice Barrès,* p. 162.
15. Quoted from Maurras by H. Massis, *Barrès et nous,* (Paris: Plon, 1962), p. 37.
16. "Leroy-Gigot-Picard," *La Cocarde,* Jan. 10, 1885.
17. H. Massis, *Barrès et nous,* p. 48.
18. Boisdeffre, *Barrès parmi nous,* (Paris: Plon, 1969), p. 76.
19. *Mes Cahiers,* vol. 2, pp. 228, 242.
20. *Ibid.,* p. 108.
21. Boisdeffre, *Maurice Barrès,* (Paris: Classiques du XXᵉ siècle, 1962), p. 95.
22. The title of the final chapter of *Les Amitiés françaises.*
23. See *Les Lézardes sur la maison,* (Paris: Sansot, 1904), pp. 30, 38, 39, 53. This work is a selection of articles published in *La Patrie* and *Le Gaulois* between July 1902 and January 1904.

24. See C. Stewart Doty, "Maurice Barrès," Ph.D. Diss., Ohio State University, 1964, pp. 72-73.

25. Pierre Baral, "Barrès parlementaire" in *Actes du Colloque Maurice Barrès,* p. 154.

26. Boisdeffre, *Barrès parmi nous,* p. 141.

27. *Ibid.,* p. 165. See also the Epilogue "Fascism, Pétainism and Gaullism" in R. Soucy, *Fascism in France; the Case of Maurice Barrès.*

28. Attested to by Maurras in Boisdeffre, *Barrès parmi nous,* pp. 178-79.

29. *Mes Cahiers,* vol. 6, pp. 137-38.

30. Quoted by Pierre Moreau, *Barrès,* (Paris: Desclée de Brouwer, 1970), p. 19.

31. *Mes Cahiers,* vol. 1, pp. 37-38.

32. *Ibid.,* vol. 5, p. 329.

33. *Ibid.,* p. 191.

34. *Ibid.,* p. 85.

35. *Ibid.,* p. 57.

36. His interest in Joan of Arc has been traced back as early as 1890 — Z. Sternhell, *Maurice Barrès et le nationalisme français,* p. 230.

37. *Mes Cahiers,* vol. 7, p. 290.

38. See Barrès' articles in *Chronique de la Grande Guerre,* vol. 1, pp. 15-87.

39. R.S. Bourne, "Maurice Barrès and the Youth of France," *Atlantic Monthly,* CXIV (Sept. 1914), pp. 394-99.

40. *Mes Cahiers,* vol. 11, p. 198.

41. He was generally in favor of Clemenceau's support of Wilson — see Guy Tosi, "Maurice Barrès regarde d'Annunzio" in *Actes du Colloque Maurice Barrès,* p. 224.

42. *Mes Cahiers,* vol. 13, pp. 107-08.

43. *Ibid.,* vol. 14, p. 155.

Chapter Two

1. Whom we shall call Philippe, even though he is not baptized until *Le Jardin de Bérénice.*

2. *Examen des trois romans idéologiques.*

3. The similarities between Barrès and Bergson are first pointed out by Jaurès, who criticizes them both severely. These similarities are, however, a product of parallel thinking rather than "influence," since Barrès denies having read Bergson until much later — see H. Massis, *Barrès et nous,* p. 52. The same is true of Nietzsche, who is unknown to Barrès before 1902 — see P. Moreau, *Barrès,* p. 16.

4. As I. M. Frandon points out in "Barrès et la création poétique" in *Actes du Colloque Maurice Barrès,* p. 293.

5. R. Soucy, *Fascism in France; the Case of Maurice Barrès*, p. 73.
6. Enzo Caramaschi, "Maurice Barrès et Venise" in *Actes du Colloque Maurice Barrès*, pp. 265-84.
7. *Un Homme libre* in *Le Culte du Moi*, (Paris: Plon, 1966), p. 138.
8. R. Soucy, *Fascism in France; the Case of Maurice Barrès*, pp. 70-71, 116.
9. *Le Jardin de Bérénice*, p. 357.
10. *Ibid.*, p. 350.
11. A notion most recently refined by A. Koestler's *The Ghost in the Machine*.

Chapter Three

1. His changing attitudes are reflected in the collection *Taine et Renan; pages perdues*, ed. Giraud (Paris: Editions Bossard, 1922).
2. *Ibid.*, p. 39.
3. Reproduced as "Le Frein couvert d'écume" in *N'importe où hors du monde*, (Paris: Plon, 1958), pp. 111-66.
4. It will later be easy to explain this tendency through the theory of uprootedness. The Jews, being attached to no homeland have developed intellect at the expense of feeling.
5. See Z. Sternhell, *Maurice Barrès et le nationalisme français*, p. 182.

Chapter Four

1. H. Massis, *Barrès parmi nous*, pp. 61-62.
2. *Mes Cahiers*, vol. 1, p. 11.
3. For a judicious comparison of Burdeau and Bouteiller, see Maurice Davanture, "Barrès, Burdeau et Bouteiller" in *Actes du Colloque Maurice Barrès*, pp. 33-44.
4. That Barrès thoroughly misunderstands Kant and judges his philosophy most unfairly is well attested to by H. Miéville, *La Pensée de Maurice Barrès*, (Paris: Editions de la Nouvelle Revue Critique, 1934), p. 118; P. Ouston, *The Imagination of Maurice Barrès*, (University of Toronto Press, 1974), p. 208; and A. Thibaudet, *La Vie de Maurice Barrès*, (Paris: Editions de la Nouvelle Revue Française, 1921), p. 176.
5. *Les Déracinés*, (Lausanne: La Guilde du Livre, 1960), p. 121.
6. Letter no. XXXIII, part I.
7. P. Ouston, *The Imagination of Maurice Barrès*, p. 48.
8. Z. Sternhell, *Maurice Barrès et le nationalisme français*, p. 155.
9. *Ibid.*, p. 88.
10. *Mes Cahiers*, vol. 1, p. 40.
11. "La Voie du peuple et le proscrit," *Le Courrier de l'Est*, 31 Aug. 1890.

12. Mermeix (pseud. Gabriel Terrail), *Les Coulisses du Boulangisme,* (Paris: Léopold Cerf, 1890).

Chapter Five

1. Quoted by Abba Eban, *My People; the Story of the Jews,* (New York, Random House, 1968), p. 297.

2. In 1889, Déroulède had accosted the troops returning from the funeral of President Félix Faure, urging them to storm the Elysée Palace. Ill-planned, ill-timed, and ill-executed, his scheme never had a chance.

Chapter Six

1. *Les Taches d'encre,* no. 1, 5 Nov. 1889.
2. "La prochaine Constitution," *Le Courrier de l'Est,* 21 Feb. 1889.
3. "France et Allemagne," *Le Courrier de l'Est,* 11 Apr. 1891.
4. "Pas de dictature," *La Cocarde,* 30 Dec. 1894.
5. "Il ne faillait pas émigrer," *Le Figaro,* 16 Nov. 1901.
6. *Mes Cahiers,* vol. 3, pp. 117-19.
7. Boisdeffre, *Barrès parmi nous,* p. 117.
8. Tharaud, *Mes années chez Barrès,* (Paris: Plon, 1928), p. 252.

Chapter Seven

1. H. Miéville, *La Pensée de Maurice Barrès,* p. 71.
2. Enzo Caramaschi, "Maurice Barrès et Venise," p. 277.
3. The characters are from the first story of the collection "Un amateur d'âmes."
4. Of "Un amour de Thulé."
5. See Jean Levaillant, "Barrès et la rêverie" in *Actes du Colloque Maurice Barrès,* especially pp. 202-04.
6. *Mes Cahiers,* vol. 3, p. 71.
7. Enzo Caramaschi claims that the pages on Tiepolo are in reality among the best that have been written on the state of mind of the end-of-the-century decadent — see his article "Maurice Barrès et Venise," p. 274.
8. Whose real name was Garabed.
9. *Le Voyage de Sparte,* (Paris: Plon, 1954), p. 171.
10. None of the influences in question are French. In the case of Claude Gellée, from his native Lorraine; Barrès seeks to minimize the foreign Italian influence — see Borreli, "Barrès et la psychologie de l'art" in *Actes du colloque Maurice Barrès,* p. 89.

Chapter Eight

1. P. Moreau, *Barrès*, p. 59.
2. "A la cathédrale," *Le Courrier de l'Est,* 9 Apr. 1892.
3. See Castex, "Barrès, collaborateur du *Voltaire*" in *Actes du Colloque Maurice Barrès,* p. 56.
4. Duhourcau, *La Voix intérieure de Maurice Barrès,* p. 225.
5. "La Foi en sociologie," *La Cocarde,* 26 Oct. 1894.
6. P. Moreau, *Barrès,* p. 66.
7. Barrès has adopted this notion from Louis Ménard — see *Le Voyage de Sparte,* pp. 16-17.
8. R. Lalou, *Maurice Barrès,* (Paris: Hachette, 1950), p. 148.
9. E.g., 29 Oct. 1914, 26 Oct. 1915.
10. Moreau speaks of this as a tension between Dionysius and Apollo — "Maurice Barrès et l'Homme libre" in *Actes du Colloque Maurice Barrès,* pp. 13-14.
11. *Mes Cahiers,* vol. 13, pp. 205-07, 212-15, 215-18.
12. Miéville believes that the same anguish has led Barrès to formulate the "Culte du Moi" — *La Pensée de Maurice Barrès,* p. 221.
13. *La Colline inspirée,* ed. J. Barbier (Nancy: Berger-Levrault, 1962), p. 13. Barbier also links the three major stages of the novel with steps in Barrès' own life — "La Colline inspirée" in *Actes du Colloque Maurice Barrès,* p. 192.
14. There are numerous instances in which Barrès alters details, the better to heighten the dramatic tension and artistic truth of his work. These have been pointed out by Barbier in his excellent critical edition of *La Colline inspirée.*
15. *Les Maîtres,* (Paris: Plon, 1927), p. 49.
16. Even when it is based on a rather doubtful interpretation of a verse from St. Paul — see *La Colline inspirée (édition critique),* p. 149, no. 6.
17. This will be the symbolism of the *Auxerre Sibyll.*
18. For a different assessment, see Henri Gouhier, "Pascal et Barrès" in *Actes du Colloque Maurice Barrès,* pp. 309-29.
19. E.g., "Le Culte de Jeanne d'Arc," *Echo de Paris,* 9 May 1915.
20. *Le Génie du Rhin,* (Paris: Plon, 1921), pp. 213-24.
21. "The foam-flecked bit" in *N'importe où hors du monde,* pp. 111-66.
22. H. Miéville, *La Pensée de Maurice Barrès,* p. 194.

Chapter Nine

1. *Les diverses familles spirituelles de la France,* (Paris: Plon, 1930), p. iv.

2. R. Graves, *Goodbye to all that,* (Penguin: London, 1960), p. 158.

3. Soucy claims that Barrès takes for granted a double standard of morality — generosity towards one's kinsmen, defiance towards aliens. *Fascism in France; the Case of Maurice Barrès,* p. 184.

4. *Les diverses familles spirituelles de la France,* p. 55.

5. H. Massis, *Barrès et nous,* p. 53.

6. *Pour la haute intelligence française,* (Paris: Plon, 1925), p. 23.

7. Sternhell shows himself aware of the limitations of Barrès' internationalism when he says of *Le Génie du Rhin* that Barrès goes to Strasbourg to announce to the world that Europe will be remade along the lines of French nationalism. *Maurice Barrès et le nationalisme français,* p. 358.

8. See "L'Homme préhistorique," *Mes Cahiers,* vol. 13.

Chapter Ten

1. *Mes Cahiers,* vol. 10, p. 282.

2. In *La Faute de l'Abbé Mouret,* especially.

3. E.g., the Franciscans — *Faut-il authoriser les congrégations?,* (Paris: Plon, 1924), p. 119.

4. Later scholarship has confirmed this tentative judgment.

5. *Une enquête aux pays du Levant,* (Paris, Plon, 1923), vol. 1, p. 309.

6. *N'importe où hors du monde,* pp. 167-78, 239-44.

7. Reproduced in *Mes Cahiers,* vol. 4, pp. 225-67, and in *N'importe où hors du monde,* pp. 47-74.

8. *La Nouvelle Héloïse,* premiere partie, lettre LV.

Chapter Eleven

1. Boisdeffre, *Barrès parmi nous,* p. 155.

2. In modern times, Giono appears to be one of the rare exceptions.

3. Boisdeffre, *Barrès parmi nous,* p. 155.

4. "Figures nouvelles, M. Henry Houssaye," *La France,* 10 Mar. 1886.

5. R. Soucy, *Fascism in France; the Case of Maurice Barrès,* pp. 266-67.

6. P. Ouston, *The Imagination of Maurice Barrès,* p. 256.

7. Causing Boisdeffre to "invent" a quotation, which he then discovers to be substantially correct, "Ah! si j'avais pensé l'Europe comme j'ai pensé la Lorraine" — *Maurice Barrès,* p. 88.

8. H. Miéville, *La Pensée de Maurice Barrès,* p. 213.

Selected Bibliography

PRIMARY SOURCES

L'Oeuvre de Maurice Barrès. 20 vols. Paris, Au Club de l'Honnête Homme, 1965-1968.
Chronique de la Grande Guerre. 14 vols. Paris, Plon. 1931-1939.
Mes Cahiers. 14 vols. Paris, Plon, 1929-1948.
Un Homme libre. Bibliothèque Nationale, Manuscrits, N.a.fr. 11728.
Les Amitiés françaises. Bibliothèque Nationale, Manuscrits, N.a.fr. 22967.

SECONDARY SOURCES

Actes du Colloque Maurice Barrès organisé par la Faculté des lettres et des sciences humaines de l'Université de Nancy. Annales de l'Est, 1963. A stimulating collection of articles by various hands on Barrès and his work.
DE BOISDEFFRE, P. *Maurice Barrès.* Paris, Classiques du XXᵉ siècle, Editions Universitaires, 1962. Boisdeffre is always interesting, and here gives a worthwhile introductory study of Barrès and his work.
DOMENACH, J. M. *Barrès par lui-même.* Paris, Editions du Seuil, 1954. Another very useful introductory study, containing excerpts from Barrès' work.
OUSTON, P. *The Imagination of Maurice Barrès.* University of Toronto Press, 1974. Basically a study of the use of poetry and evocation in the elaboration of Barrès' ideas. Provides a very useful overview of his work.
SOUCY, R. *Fascism in France; the Case of Maurice Barrès.* University of California Press, 1972. Discusses the elements of Fascism in Barrès' work. Detailed, though perhaps a little harsh on Barrès.
STERNHELL, Z. *Maurice Barrès et le nationalisme française.* Paris Armand Colin, 1972. A very careful study of Barrès' political stances and fortunes from 1884 to 1902. Makes abundant use of Barrès' unpublished articles.
ZARACH, H. *Bibliographie Barrèsienne.* Paris, Presses Universitaires de France, 1951. Although now over twenty years old, this bibliography is still a necessity for anyone undertaking work on Barrès.

Index